GROWN·UP FAST

A TRUE STORY OF TEENAGE LIFE IN SUBURBAN AMERICA

BETSY ISRAEL

POSEIDON PRESS

NEW YORK • LONDON • TORONTO • SYDNEY • TOKYO

Published by Poseidon Press
A Division of Simon & Schuster Inc.
Simon & Schuster Building
Rockefeller Center
1230 Avenue of the Americas
New York, NY 10020

POSEIDON PRESS is a registered trademark of Simon & Schuster Inc.

Designed by SNAP·HAUS GRAPHICS
Manufactured in the United States of America

10   9   8   7   6   5   4   3   2   1

Library of Congress Cataloging-in-Publication Data

Israel, Betsy
    Grown-up fast : a true story of teenage life in surburban America
Betsy Israel.
    p.   cm.
    1. Israel, Betsy   .   2. Teenagers—United States—
Biography.   I. Title.
HQ796.I77 1988
305.2'35'0924—dc19
ISBN 0-671-63533-6

Portions of the article "Alleged Baby Seller" are reprinted by permission of
New York Post copyright 1978.

Portions of the song "Little Green," © 1967, 1975 by Joni Mitchell, are
reprinted courtesy of Siquomb Publishing Corp.

Portions of the song "A Case of You," © 1971, 1975 by Joni Mitchell, are
reprinted courtesy of Joni Mitchell Publishing Corp.

For my parents and sisters
and for Alex Greenfield

Although the story told in this book is entirely true, the names and identifying details of the characters other than myself have been changed. Most of the events reported took place when many of the persons portrayed were in their teens. In telling this story, I had no wish to embarrass these individuals or to intrude upon their present lives.

1 9 8 5

The man who had written "Stress and Sex: The Truth about Pleasure under Pressure" was saying that I had fucked with his prose. It was 9:07 A.M. I was standing in my office with my sneakers still on. He was reviewing, without pausing for breath, cuts made to the lubrication paragraph. I gave him credit: He knew how to catch an editor off guard. He did not know how to write.

"Bob," I said, "please calm down. We'll go through the whole thing together, word by word. Just let me find the galley, okay?" I dropped the phone. My desk, which I had been seated at mere hours before, was a mess—manuscripts and message slips scattered in the style of a welfare office bombing. I removed one sneaker at a time and got some coffee. I began, with shape as a guideline, to make some piles. From one of them came the disembodied whine of the writer. I shouted, "Bob, please hold." The coffee spilled. 9:10: It promised to be a long morning.

At 9:14 Tammi from Art appeared to lecture on "type widows that are threatening the new design scheme." Behind her trudged the Arts editor clutching a bran muffin. The editor lay down on my couch without explanation. Tammi said, "Look. Your department is fucking us on column cuts." I looked out the window. A car skidded and hit something. I looked back at Tammi and said, "Is there a way this could wait until later?" Tammi said that this was possible, for a few minutes maybe, and left. My colleague sat up on the couch and I looked down to find three phone lines lit. Bob, on one, was saying, "Female orgasm, whether or not you wish to acknowledge this, is primarily a mental event, which leads us to certain inescapable conclusions."

"Bob," I said, sighing, "we really shouldn't be dealing with content at this point," but Jennifer, my assistant, interrupted.

"Writer lunch at Russian Tea Room," she announced, twirling a strand of silver beads the size of golf balls. "12:30. Ashley. Your fave."

My lunch date's name was actually John. He was Southern and had once, kidding around, said "Thank you, ma'am" to

Jennifer, who from then on called him Ashley. The Arts editor departed my couch, leaving the muffin, like a large brown mushroom, on the floor. Jennifer winked and followed. Flipping my desk calendar to December 15, I said, "Bob, I know this is terrible, but it looks like I've got a meeting."

On cue, ten editors wandered in, a blur of sparkly pink stretch pants and blue Hellenic-theme coffee containers. They arranged themselves in a circle around the muffin as if to conduct a séance. One of the Trend editors raised her pen.

"I think we should look seriously at the death of the anorexic sex symbol," she said. "You know, like, examine the tyranny of Twiggy, because personally I feel kind of like I was fucked over by Twiggy, conceptually I mean, and I think every generation just has its Twiggys, updated."

No response came immediately to mind. An editor from Health and Fitness, to my relief, nodded and said, "Yeah. I think I can see this. It's like we're seeing, like, a new voluptuousness," but I was listening to a siren, an ambulance trapped and yelping between cars out on the avenue. I remembered the skid and imagined blood, the sounds of a pedestrian screaming as her limp body was heaved onto the stretcher. "I've got the slug," the Arts associate screamed suddenly. "The slug is: Curves Ahead!"

The ambulance passed. I focused again on the group and said, "It might fly." I sat up, said to Jennifer, "Find possible pegs for this," then moved the discussion to the coming month's lineup. We reviewed progress on "By Food Obsessed" and "White-Collar Jesus Freaks." We argued over the "ineffable style"/fashion tie-in, debating for half an hour whether or not Marie Antoinette was the first woman to have died for her ineffable style. No consensus was reached.

One hour later I stood to tie my trench coat, missing all its buttons, with a brown silk scarf I'd found beneath the desk. "See ya at three," I said to Jennifer. "Regards to Ashley," she said, sounding British, and I stepped quickly past the girls sorting reject blush outside of Beauty.

It was chilly in the lobby; strips of rain carpet stretched out to the door to form a pointillist canvas of heel prints. Dodging blondes balancing pasta salads, dark-haired women wearing bracelets so wide they seemed to have medical use, I threw my body against the revolving door and stepped out onto the street. People walked with heads down so that you saw only scalp. People in cars slapped steering wheels, mouthing *shit*. The sky was ice clear, as unforgiving as a mirror.

In the Russian Tea Room, 100-proof vodka spreading out through my chest like a liniment, I described to John-Ashley "The Relationship That Wouldn't Die," a humor piece we wanted for an issue in spring. I went through the piece in some detail, moving my hands in circular patterns to convey enthusiasm. Yawning, Ashley leaned forward to observe, "You're wearing lipstick," then let his foot drop groggily onto mine. Things, as they had in the past with this writer, degenerated quickly. I stabbed a blintz on his plate. He tore some black bread and fed me the crust. Three vodka shots later, I rested my head on the red leather banquette, my hair static-tinged, spreading out to suggest an early Marilyn Monroe, curls plush against the satin of a calendar backdrop. I was drunk. 2:30: I sensed a long afternoon.

Walking down Fifty-seventh Street, Ashley explained that he planned to make his way quickly crosstown to Madison somewhere near Seventy-second Street. He said that he'd think about doing the piece, added that he was late and then stepped firmly off the curb at Sixth Avenue.

Nodding, I tried on behalf of the magazine to present a brief, enticing summary of the piece he might write. But it was cold out. I'd been drinking. What I said was, "On my way back to the office, I think I'll stop for some coffee and maybe try to see the tree at Rockefeller Center." Stepping down off the curb alongside him, I added, "We're heading into an extremely bad close. I have two free-lance pieces untyped. I've been so goddamned frantic I seem barely to have noticed it's December."

Ashley hunched his shoulders, glanced at his watch, then at his feet. Pausing, I said, "We're really hoping that you'll take this piece on." Ashley said, "Okay. I'll do it, but I have to go *now*." And so we walked our separate ways on Sixth. Wispy clouds thin as cigarette smoke stretched out across the sky, end to end. The brown silk scarf had disappeared.

On the sunken skating rink at Rockefeller Center, life proceeded as usual. I stood a minute watching the spindly girls in furry red velvet pass delicately by the guys in airtight jeans. I bought some coffee and, sipping it, walked slowly through the promenade, past the mothers demanding smiles, the packs of well-groomed Japanese voluntarily smiling. "Silent Night," a tinny disco version, was piped in and I sang along, summoning up the countless photos of me in this scene at Winter Festival—the holiday families more socially acceptable than mine had called Christmas. Mentally arranging the photos by year, I composed a Kodak commercial about a girl as she grew: in 1968, a bulky red stocking cap and messy braids; in '72, no trace of eyebrow, arms folded across a leotard worn two weeks straight without changing. In 1977—but I had arrived already at Fifth Avenue.

I pictured my office, the bomb site. I pictured a trail of pink message slips starting in the reception area and, like crumbs dropped in the woods, leading back to my phone. At least three, I guessed, would be from Bob concerning mental orgasm. Unfastening the top of the coffee container, I said, "Fuck it," turned and walked back past the white wire angels toward the tree. Perhaps, I thought, I'd turn up in some family portrait as—and here's the slug!—A Stranger in the Frame. But this reminded me of work; I forgot it and instead blurred my vision so that the bright gold and black stores, the tinselly angels softened to resemble a Vaseline-lensed ad, the kind one might find in a fragile old *Life* of my mother's.

But this reverie was interrupted. There were three people in front of me, a man and a woman holding hands with a girl of about seven, and they kept getting in my way. No matter how I tried to pass, they spread out hand in hand across the sidewalk. They insisted on singing. They were, quite obviously, from the suburbs. I considered pushing past, commenting loudly about bridge-and-tunnel people out of sync with the city, but I did not.

Trying to keep off their heels, I recalled special city days of my own—me on a bench to the right, begging my mother to do the dance routine she'd done once on Broadway; me in the Librairie de France, to my left, pretending to read *Huis Clos* as the French class trip left without me. The girl in front of me now wore a purple down coat that matched her mother's. The father had on penny loafers. "Yes," I said out loud, "these people belong here, with the Japanese cameras and the folk art store where they sell dolls made in Alabama out of straw." Some guy passing on my left shot me a look. The little girl skipped across to the Librairie de France. I looked at her reflection in the window.

I wanted to check my watch but stared straight ahead at the girl. I heard the mother say, "There it is," one finger raised to the tree. The father pulled a pipe from his pocket. The girl smiled, tiny teeth the size of corn kernels appearing in storefront glass and then vanishing. It seemed that I had moved unnaturally close. I said, This is not that interesting.

You have to go. But when the family walked on, I felt myself follow. This is ridiculous, I said, Get the fuck back to work. Still I stayed with them. Ahead of me the crowds seem to part and the ice to rise up out of the earth, a busy oval moon. Just as quickly they reconverged, swallowing the family, and I stood there.

I said, You're drunk and sentimental. One tends, in such a state, to free-associate: I thought of Winter Festival and I thought next of marzipan, my sisters or my grandmother; I imagine old Christmas pictures and feel drawn to a girl on the street. I tried to associate from a Rolodex to page proofs. 3:00: The afternoon was shrinking. I turned to go.

But at the edge of the crowd, at the tip of the last store off Fiftieth Street, stood the girl in the purple coat. She was posing for her father, hugging herself like a fur-coat model on late-night TV, tilting her head, changing angle, rotating, so that very slowly she came face to face with me. The girl continued to smile. I tried, in the spirit of things, to smile along, but a chill like a spasm raced up my spine, skipping across vertebrae to the shoulders, forcing a sound like *oh* to leak from my lips.

There was coffee lapping my sleeve in a small muddy wave. I shivered. I took a breath. I looked again at this girl and saw in her all the Kodak photos arranged to make one, for it was in this frame my own face that looked back—wide brown eyes and little teeth—the face of Christmas 1966 having its picture retaken. Bizarre memories began flying by in my mind to a Frank Sinatra song about autumn. I remembered being eight and obsessed with Hollywood monsters, especially The Mummy, who'd been buried alive—my second greatest fear, following a possible guerilla assault launched by spiders. Falling asleep at night, I would imagine human sounds receding as the coffin filled with sand. At the Metropolitan Museum I'd ask my father about live burial, about what The Mummy, understandably upset, had said upon his unveiling. My father, leading me off to study canopic jars, would always say, "You'll just have to imagine it for yourself."

I had no idea why I was thinking about this on my lunch break, except that I seemed, somehow, to be hearing the sound I had once imagined—an ancient arcing moan that stirred deep in the intestines and grew louder as it found its way up my throat in two words. I said, "My daughter."

This girl, I said again, could have been the child handed over one April day eight years earlier—a teenage disaster hidden at the time by thick blankets, rarely mentioned as years passed and in 1985, I liked to think, forgotten.

The family walked on. Allowing one or two white-haired men, a few secretaries as buffers, I followed them across Fifth, past Saks, their every move heightened, quivering as if photographed for a Japanese art film. On Fifty-fifth Street the father took the girl's hand, folding it carefully, like a tiny origami rose, into his own; turning onto Madison, the mother unfurled a tissue so that it flapped in the wind like a flag.

By Sixtieth Street all saliva had evaporated. My chest ached. I threw the coffee, which had left me smelling vaguely of coleslaw, into a trash can and missed. I tried again and missed. When I looked up, the father, to my right, had opened the doors of a brown Toyota. In front of me the mother, clasping the girl's shoulders, said, "It's time." Directly to my left stood Ashley-John, the writer.

Ashley waved and walked over, a look on his face like the one you flash a guy whose fly has seriously opened in public.

"Hey," he said, grabbing my arm near the wet spot, "how the hell did you get all the way here?"

ONE

On the South Shore local out of Manhattan, Massapequa is stop number eight, toward the end of the roll call beginning in Rockville Centre and ending in Babylon, placed perfectly, if you grew up there, between the borders of the known world. At the far end, beyond even Queens, lay New York City, where my mother had once lived in the thin graceful light of an early color film, sleeping to the muted clank of a dumbwaiter, waking to lean romantically out over a soot-covered air shaft. On the near side was Babylon, a town much like Massapequa but famous for the way conductors called it last—"and Baa-ba-lawn"—like old sportscasters who'd taken up barbershop harmonies in retirement.

Massapequa was then a suburban town of its time, an area of summer homes and vacant lots transformed after the war into a residential bedroom community. Hopeful city emigrants were drawn to it and to surrounding towns like Amityville for the usual reasons: the slightly exaggerated rumors of good schools; the white beaches (in terms both of sand and skin color); the quarter-acre lots nonexistent in the row-house neighborhoods of Queens, and all just one hour out of the city, an ad might have read, at prices far below those of fancy mock-Tudor towns like Great Neck to the north or the older, amply lawned communities like Hewlett and Cedarhurst to the west.

My parents, sitting one evening at a fold-out kitchen table in their Bayside, Queens, apartment, took out a map and a compass and drew a circle with a radius of forty miles out from the city. Massapequa, the last town in Nassau County on the South Shore, was the farthest acceptable point.

My mother, then a slender twenty-five-year-old dancer, was the only child of a Kansas-born potter and a Cuban choreographer. She came to Long Island by way of their Upper West Side apartment, the High School of Performing Arts and chorus parts in Broadway shows. I imagined her early life photographed in CinemaScope, constructed of scenes I had memorized from the cast album photos of *Fiorello!*, *The Most*

Happy Fella and *The Pajama Game*. She seemed to me innately equipped for her profession, possessing naturally the broad smile and good posture others exaggerated on stage. And if her hair was known to travel the entire spectrum of red, according to show, every other theatrical attribute was her own: Her teeth had always been straight, her cheekbones high and round, and her fingers long and white and kept bare except for the plain gold band that matched my father's.

He was a World War II air force veteran, then as beautiful and dark as a star himself—Tyrone Power, it was most often agreed, although if you squinted you could see young Jack Lemmon. He'd grown up the only son of Orthodox Jewish parents in a meticulously swept half a house near Coney Island. There, according to jagged-edged snapshots, he had spent his early life reading serious books while holding his forehead up with one finger, or sailing on Sheepshead Bay with girls inexplicably wearing snoods.

During the early 1950s my father worked as a copywriter at an ad agency located near the studio where my mother took ballet class. They met at a bus stop or at a children's theater production both were involved in, or possibly at a Burt Lancaster movie about pirates. The ensuing courtship possessed what would later seem to me the signatures of the prehistoric New York world: My father rode the subway from Brooklyn to the West Eighties for a nickel, then escorted my mother to musicals starring Mary Martin and then later to parties where young artistic couples stood in the bathtub, due to lack of space. On the way home, at a dizzying 11:30, they'd stroll in deserted Central Park, feeding pigeons, discussing "The Age of Anxiety," an important new ballet by Jerome Robbins.

He was ten years older; she, the child of artist-socialists, was most severely not Jewish. It was, at least from the standpoint of my father's family, a less than popular relationship.

Still, after countless scenes in which Jewish relatives exited rooms en masse like UN delegates staging a walkout, after lengthy kitchen diatribes and slammed telephones on Shabbat, the couple held a poorly attended civil ceremony, spent a week on Cape Cod and decided soon after to buy a house, one with a yard large enough for wooden swings and puppet stages, badminton nets, vegetables, lilacs, English gardens in miniature—with all of the things my mother considered essential.

In August 1958 my father's oldest friend, Benny Mortenson, having drawn a compass circle of his own, moved from Brooklyn to Massapequa. He had found a house in Nassau Shores, one of the waterfront communities that on a map jut into the Great South Bay like the teeth of a key. The following month I was born, and the month after, Benny, who had become my fake-uncle, turned up a plot of land nearby his own. For just under $17,000, my father purchased the land and commissioned a red-shingled three-floor split-level with a sloping roof and bay window. For just under $20, he bought a monthly LIRR commutation ticket to the city, and in fake-Uncle Benny's Oldsmobile, crammed alongside my fake-Aunt Ruth and two fake-cousins, we drove out on Sunrise Highway to Massapequa and to Moccasin Lane, past the wooden Indian statue of Realtor "Big Chief" Lewis, faithful bison cub at his side, past the blinking green arrow pointing the way to White's department store and drive-in and to the famed Massapequa Zoo—a tiny amusement park then cashing in on the postwar baby boom but soon to be torn down. Those born at the close of the 1950s would later swear they remembered the Massapequa Zoo vividly, as surely as they remembered the day Kennedy was killed.

• • •

There are the usual pictures of this time in the suburbs, approximately 300 variations of each one.

My mother poses the first year on the rocky moonscape that was our lawn, a baby carriage like a small European car out in front of her, a bulky plaid McCall's-pattern coat hiding her second pregnancy. Her hair is bright orange, her lips the shade of red one might find in a period propaganda shot depicting how normal life will be after the A-bomb.

I pose with my first sister, a tiny translucent baby who smiles in spite of the way I let her tip over on my parents' bed, or because she has not yet learned that her name is Gwyneth Rose.

As Gwyn becomes a more substantial playmate, I hide with her behind newly made tables, dressers and chairs, our tiny bodies swathed in retired costumes: blue ruffled princess skirts, cone hats built up with plastic fruit, genie pants made from the same silky material as the living-room curtains. A white-and-salmon-colored TV looms like a robot's head in the background, and we stare out at it. Or we stare up at the old oaks that line the gravel-filled street like giants' shins.

There are often other children staring up, and dogs, usually collies. One year in the early sixties, the children are bigger than the dogs. And that, at around the time the streets were paved, is when real life seemed to begin.

As with most suburban children, our first basic belief concerned our house and its occupation of a superior position in the universe. There were, even at a young age, distinctions to be made. Fake-Aunt Ruth often said that Massapequa was inherently better than places like Levittown, where the houses were so alike the design might have been lifted from a museum exhibit called "Uniformity and Mid-Century Man."

And unlike the comparable areas of nearby Seaford and Free-port ("fishing towns, commercial," said Aunt Ruth), unlike Massapequa Park (across the tracks, where there were identical brick houses and few trees), Nassau Shores had a history of being only a pretty place on the water; *Architectural Record,* it was said, had voted it "Best-Planned Summer Community of 1934."

But these distinctions—no matter how nastily you spit out the *t* in Levittown—easily blurred. Each South Shore town looked basically the same: Long Island Rail Road tracks through the center, Sunrise Highway alongside, and Merrick Road parallel to that, a quarter of a mile down toward the bay. And our block, even with its trees and varied houses, seemed similar to one in Massapequa Park, where, as I'd pictured it, retired navy men sat on cracked brick stoops, spitting alongside sons tattooed at young ages.

Actually what I'd noticed was this: Mothers on our block did not work and wore aprons over skirts at all times. Fathers, whether they worked for insurance companies or at Merrick Road gas stations, seemed interchangeable. They left, waving, in morning, and returned, waving, in afternoon. Most parents shouted openly in the presence of children and all had names that ended in an *i* or an *o* or began with *Mc.* By the time I'd reached age five, our prized distinctions had become wobbly. What was distinct, I'd slowly sensed, was us.

Unlike any mother I had ever met, ours had a job—as a part-time ballet teacher at a Merrick Road studio run by a former New York City Ballet star. Dressed in a black leotard and a red plaid skirt she'd let us zipper, her hair tied loosely back with a piece of green velvet, she spent her mornings making doll clothes and cookies and afternoons hopping around the kitchen with us, humming, counting out the rhythms of the combinations she would teach in her 4:30 class.

Unlike any father anywhere, as far as I knew, ours was around to watch. In 1962 he'd quit his advertising job "on principle"—my mother's code phrase for anti-Semitism—and had not taken on another full time. He worked with fake-Uncle Benny, who designed steel for buildings, or freelanced in the city as a copywriter. At home he shouted behind the master bedroom door about money, painted our portraits in watercolor, and drove the family off to visit grandparents —who were not, it went without saying, the typical sets of two who sat, nodding, in lawn chairs—then back home to prepare the fish he had captured in the bay and horribly skinned earlier that week.

On some childhood nights he drove to Queens College, where he was finishing the degree he'd abandoned for the war. In his absence we watched "Lost in Space," cuddled with our mother, and ate anything but fish.

On winter Sundays we ate pancakes and sausage in front of the TV—"Ed Sullivan Breakfast Night"—and later watched our parents waltz around the living room to Benny Goodman or Bunny Berrigan, variations of "Benny," we assumed, being the most common names of their era.

Summers, we floated out after dinner to jump for lightning bugs or to roll to the car for a trip to the library. Because of the trees, it got dark early in Nassau Shores, even in summer. From the backseat I'd watch blue shadows drop like hats onto bay-window bushes, the smoky black-and-white hush of muffled TVs announcing night. Many neighbors had ceramic dwarfs on their lawns, plastic deer tucked in bushes. At dusk, lightning bugs appearing, then melting, like the stars on the plug-in painting at the savings bank, it was hard to be sure that the deer weren't real, or that South Merrick Road was not a long green passage in a forest my father had painted. I held on to Gwyn as the car crawled through it, imagining the leaves and shadows tight around the car like moss. Nothing, as I pictured it, not dead fish, not the neighbors who never went to the library, could get inside.

The mid-1960s brought ritualized begging for shorter skirts, Batman and elementary school.

Like the five others in town, Unqua School was over-crowded and the sidewalks leading up to it were always jammed. Walking slowly with Gwyn, attached to my mitten by a large safety pin in her sleeve, I'd study my peers for relevant Bat insignia and acceptably short hems. Our neighbor Marie-Ellen Scarparelli, who was taller and wore rings she got out of gum machine capsules, served as my model. Like other girls, she dressed for school in pointy white vinyl boots and tiny purple skirts. She rode on bikes with an older brother and, like all girls I knew, wore cross necklaces featuring the man Gwyn called "the baby cheese." They seemed to exist inside a world of mysterious privilege, these girls, a magical neon-lit world in which TV dinners and pink store-bought clothes were as common as bedtime stories. But most days the crowd on Unqua Road would move, we'd reach school, and for the moment I'd forget all trace of difference.

Inside the school we were, as a group, studying what was known as "Our Indian Heritage." This involved perfecting glue-and-sparkle portraits of Indian heroes and constructing shoe-box dioramas we called "Meet the Swingin' Sioux" or "Adobe A-go-go." On lunch breaks, playground aides supervised the building of teepees from "twigs and stones indigenous to the area." Back at home, our mother had framed my macaroni-shell Sacajawea to hang proudly alongside Gwyn's

"Hopi Girl with Long Nails" collage. Everyone, even Marie-Ellen, was at work on the Plains Indian unit. There was a sense of community.

In 1966, however, in the second grade, life seemed to become serious, possibly threatening in a way no amount of Indian bonding could conceal.

One afternoon everyone in the class, with the exception of a boy named Barry Rosenblum and myself, got up and left the room, climbing aboard special minibuses parked outside. Miss Picarini, the teacher, kneeled alongside me, rubbing my forehead as if I had fever. Barry Rosenblum shot spitballs through the end of a straw at my ear.

The following Saturday I rode my bike down the block and saw Marie-Ellen Scarparelli, who, because she'd felt like it, had changed her name to "Val," standing by her forsythia bush in a mini wedding dress. Val's hands were folded in prayer; her eyes were lifted toward the TV antenna. I slowed my bike to watch from behind a tree, as jealous as I'd been of her Connie Madison School of Tap 'n Ballet glitter tutus the year before. Riding home, I saw that on every lawn there was a bride-girl. They were being tucked gently into the backseats of cars by fathers, as mothers, wearing blue hats with veils, slid in alongside. I let my bike fall in our pachysandra patch and ran to my mother, who was kneeling in the English country garden.

Out of breath, I asked, "Why is Val wearing a wedding dress?" She put down her trowel, took my hands and told me about the first Holy Communion. I asked if I could please have one myself, as soon as possible. My mother rubbed my forehead as Miss Picarini had the week before.

"Sweetheart," she said, "we do not practice an organized religion, and we are certainly not Catholic. You and your sister are special, very lucky little girls. Now the other girls don't have Passover *and* Easter, just for fun, and then Winter

Festival, do they? And they don't have your lovely thick braids and beautiful big eyes either."

This was not consolation. It was, rather, like having someone confirm the presence of illness, that a vague ache in your knee on the way to school was in fact cerebral palsy: It would get worse, you would be crippled.

Further evidence of this "illness" quickly emerged. The week after Val's first Holy Communion, boys on the hot-lunch line repeatedly raised their arms as I passed, a gesture that I associated with Hitler. In Brownies, a blond girl named Denise said, "Hi, *Ju*-dy." Finally, that weekend, while driving through Amityville, we passed a group of blacks watching a car burn at the side of the road—a scene I associated with the riots that flashed on TV between "That Girl" and "Bewitched"—and arrived home to find Val, wearing new pink mini culottes, on our stoop.

"Some pickaninnies are trying to buy a house down the block," she reported, "even though Naomi, you know, my mother, said she'll sue." I compared this to the way my own father had said, "Such a move could enrich the cultural life of the neighborhood." As if considering it too, Val added, "Yup. Jews love niggers. They'll both burn in hell." I ran inside. Val, who tended simply to repeat things she had heard, shouted, "What? Do you want gum?"

Soon after, my second and last sister, Sashi Renata, was born. Gwyn and I crowded into the corner room so the baby, who looked like a rare Arabian monkey Gwyn had seen pictured in a book, would have enough space. That same week, Val stopped by because, as she explained, she'd been passing our house and had remembered that I was her age. During the course of our visit, she gave me Lik-M-Aid, the colored sugar in a packet my mother refused to have on her property, and informed me that the second half of *The Wizard of Oz* was in color. I denied it, and she said, "How many fingers do I have up?" I said, "Two," and she changed it to three. "I guess there's something wrong with your eyes," she concluded.

I did not mention these things—not the Lik-M-Aid, not the Hitler arms or "Ju-dy." Alerting my parents to danger, asking "Mom, Dad, are we and the blacks going to be killed, set on fire, by the neighbors?" might somehow have made it real, or at least something we had to discuss, rationally, as a group at dinner. We had a new baby. I was not going to spoil everything.

On Saturdays, I began to check eight times an hour to see if Val's gold dining-room drapes had parted, coming up from the sides like a ruffly theater curtain to indicate that the Scarparellis had arisen. Behind the curtains I had discovered a house like the set of a kid's TV show, filled with Beatle records, furniture that plugged in and wiggled and Barbies that cracked like knuckles when you bent them at the waist.

Unlike any other kid I'd ever met, Val was often left home by herself, or at least with her brother, who'd wander off. She knew how to bake a frozen dinner when I could not even turn on the stove. She could make a chain belt from the tops of soda cans or design mod fashions on the backs of bank deposit slips. I admired her tremendously. But she was also slightly scary. She might, because she felt like it, just stop talking. Sometimes, without warning, she'd leave the room. Realizing that she had no intention of returning, I'd run outside to look, as if through the wide end of binoculars, down to my house.

My tiny father would be cutting the grass with the rusted hand mower he wouldn't trade for one of the little cars Catholic fathers drove across their lawns. My mother tended the English garden, now so tall our house seemed to rise from behind a purple forest; my sisters fought over our Hula Hoop.

Eventually my father would whistle for me and I'd run back home, embarrassed by the way my entire family stopped to wave. No one was ever home at Val's to wave. Her mother, regardless of season, was at the Nassau Shores beach club. Her father, who worked either for an engineering firm or at a carpet store, came home, it seemed, only to sleep. I could not picture him, whatever he did, asking Val to taste the chopped liver he'd just whipped up, breaking the matzo and giving her half.

In the fourth and fifth grades the realm of Catholic privilege expanded. On certain Fridays the entire class again left early, pushing onto the little buses, leaving just me and Barry R., who moved unexpectedly one day to Syosset. Catholic girls returned some Mondays wearing strapless pumps and fishnet stockings, mini dresses made of thick paper, and "maxi coats"—amazing floor-length drapes they hung, giggling, on special hangers in the teacher's closet. They called their outfits "Confirmation clothes." In my mind, the fashion-Catholicism connection had indeed been confirmed.

One night, helping dry the dishes, I tried to get a general sense of whether or not we could expect change in our family.

"Mommy," I began, passing a Flintstones cup to Gwyn, "can you say again why we can't be Catholic?"

My mother turned off the faucet and placed soapy hands around my chin. Sighing, she said, "What are we going to do with you?"

"Let me wear a cross to ballet," I suggested. Gwyn hit my arm and my mother clasped my chin tighter. "Elizabeth Ann," she said, "don't you ever let me hear you say that in front of your father, do you understand me?"

"It can be a plain cross," I blurted. "It doesn't have to have Jesus on it." Gwyn gasped and my mother grabbed my hands, squeezing the fingers, staring at me as she would to be sure I'd washed my neck. "Now you stop," she said, and, feeling embarrassed, I turned to hit Gwyn, who started howling. My mother spanked me, in the unserious way she spanked, and walked me out of the room, repeating, "Now, you stop."

It soon became clear that the fashion-Catholicism connection extended not just to clothes but to behavior. Girls in Library Skills, girls in Art claimed suddenly to be "in love," a curious state that involved writing LUV on bare arms with Magic Marker, dancing like Goldie and Judy from "Laugh-In" and throwing slender strings of red licorice at boys, who chewed it, then spit. Val, who as far as I knew did not like boys, bought 200 strings each day on the way to school. She called it "bait."

Lines were being drawn, I sensed, between those who would throw this bait and those who would not, which was roughly to say between those who were pretty and those plain, although this was unclear. Val, for instance, wasn't classically pretty. Her forehead and nostrils were so wide, her eyes—the oriental type without exposed eyelid—so far apart, it seemed she'd been stretched. I, on the other hand, was pretty, but I was certainly not Catholic and lacked, due to ballet, the bad posture popular girls like Val had perfected. I tried to picture boys I could love, perhaps Randy and Dennis from next door, but they were ugly, they smelled of leaves, I didn't get it. I tried once again to get some sense of things from my mother.

In the car, on our way to see Mrs. Slobodian, my new private flute teacher, I mentioned the boys and Val with her licorice. My mother inhaled so deeply her chest moved. "Why is that girl in such a hurry?" she said, pumping the brake. "It's such a brief time. You'll be grown-up fast enough and then the whole thing's over. I think you should just relax and enjoy it while it lasts. Believe me, Betsy," she said as we came to a stop, "there's time for all of that later. *Much* later."

This was the first time my mother had mentioned growing up. She had sounded annoyed. I vowed that I would make it up to her. I would read books from her era—*National Velvet*, Nancy Drew solving the case of the mysterious man's clock, or something. I kissed her, hugged my flute case to my chest and ran inside.

At Val's, where I spent every afternoon of 1967 and '68, we sat in the den watching "The Munsters" and then "Gidget," playing with her poodles, She-She and Bazoom, as we waited for her mother to leave. At last Naomi, whom Val called "The Gnome," would appear behind sunglasses and a yellow-flowered bathing cap. "*Ciao,* kids," she'd say. "*Ciao,* Gnome," Val would say, and The Gnome would look puzzled, then wink, then screech out of the driveway, racing her tiny MG down to the beach club. Val would point to the basement stairs.

For a while we'd investigate the boxes from The Gnome's former life—her Patti Page records, the shriveled old hat-pin corsages Val called "orkneys." After carefully placing the orkneys back into their boxes, we'd walk into her father's workroom, where there were *Playboys*, filed by year on one side and, on the other, by hair color of Playmate. I'd promise myself that I'd go home straight after to read from *Ring of Bright Water,* a book about friendly otters I'd begun the year before. But Val would pull down a magazine, the centerfold flopping like an obscene tongue into the room, and I'd forget it. The women pictured were so bizarre—their bodies messy with fat and hair, their lips curled like an angry dog's—I could only stare, in the same way a boy my age might have stared, fascinated by the differences, aroused and slightly guilty.

Val would break the tension by letting the magazine drop. "My father is a prevert," she'd say, wiping her hands on the inch of skirt that stuck out from her tunic. "I would rather die than have my mother's chest." I'd nod and picture my own mother, who had never liked Patti Page, and my father, who had in his workroom shelves of World War II airplane models and a portrait of Franklin D. Roosevelt. It seemed very clear that they, at least my father, would kill me if the truth of my afternoons was known.

Although I had at this point certain vague ideas about sex —the rumors of girls who bled through the nipple each month; the way neighborhood boys held my head in leaves and made me say "I am a pussy"—actual facts were few. Sex, as it existed in the Scarparelli basement and probably in the homes of the flirty licorice girls at school, did not exist in ours.

In our house there were boundaries as clear as those dividing up the town at large. My parents' bedroom door was always closed and sometimes locked. You never entered without knocking, and if you happened to stroll in, finding either parent in his or her underwear, you backed out, apologizing, as quickly as you could. Both only children, my parents were accustomed to strict divisions between parent and child: We were regarded as minors with strictly enforced curfews and handmade, individually named stuffed animals. We were children who sat at the children's table at Passover, despite the fact that by the time of the second Kennedy assassination, we could barely get our legs beneath it.

One day during the fall of 1968, Miss Jackit, the gym teacher, passed folded blue dittos back through the rows, advising us to "read these in the privacy of your own homes." It was, we discovered, ripping them open on the spot, an announcement of a movie—a movie, I suspected, about the blood and the nipples.

A few nights before the movie my mother walked into our room and asked Gwyn to leave. "See ya later, little lady," Gwyn said, wiggling her rear end, which made me want to punch her. "Gwyn, please," my mother said as she moved my baton to clear a space on the bed. She took my hand and looked at me. Things grew hazy, although I remember her saying "in the form of blood," the sound of Gwyn breathing outside the door and me saying, "Blood? Are you sure?"

After this startling revelation we sat in silence. Finally my mother said, "Do you have any questions?" I had a few, possibly 400, but how could I have asked her, my mother, the person who slept in the same bed as my father and told him things? What would I say: Mom, I have seen the inside of Mr. Scarparelli's workroom? That I had, only the week before, picked the word "penitent" in Library Skills because it fell on the same page as "penis"?

My mother pushed back my bangs. "No?" she asked.

"No," I announced, returning to my diagram of photosynthesis; and so, our one and only sex talk over, she opened the door, sending Gwyn spilling onto the rug.

The night of the menstruation movie, Val's mother came to get us in the MG. I looked out to see The Gnome leaning over the steering wheel, plastic flowers from the bathing cap in her eyes, sunglasses pointing up at the edges, though it was nearly dark. She looked like a martian. I waved, hoped my mother wouldn't notice her and ran out.

We arrived in time to see the school nurse, Miss Lappe, wearing a pale blue cardigan sweater, walk onto the auditorium stage and rub her hands together. She said, "Any questions should be directed to the parent, but as the material is entirely comprehensive, there probably won't be any," then walked off.

First there was a cartoon, a Walt Disney-style short about a stick girl who lived in the woods, where she played with three fully drawn birds who were her friends. Things in the woods go along pretty well until suddenly, one day, the girl is outlined by tiny lines suggesting a glow. Two U's appear on her chest; her hips sway out. Hair, represented by darker lines, grows on her body in unlikely places. Still, the girl smiles. The birds may or may not have smiled. I personally thought she looked terrible. I also worried that she had gotten this way rather fast. The film had not explained: Did you wake up one day transformed? But the other film was starting. My peers looked as if they would rather go home and not know.

The star of the main feature was a girl from my mother's era named Betty, who had short bangs, a long plaid skirt and saddle shoes. As the film begins, Betty strolls in late to her roller-skating lesson. Other girls skate by, waving fondly, but Betty sits off to the side. Finally her teacher, a human Ken doll with a crew cut, comes over to ask Betty why she is not "participating in the activities." Betty gazes up at him, hugs herself, then smiles shyly. "Why, Coach," she says, "how thoughtful of you to inquire. It is because I am still menstruating." It was impossible to hear what Ken said in response, because nearly every member of the audience had collapsed in laughter. "This chick is hopeless," someone shouted, and it became instant law that if someone asked "What are you doing?" you replied, "Why, Coach, how thoughtful of you to inquire."

It was raining when, after several interruptions, the Betty movie ended. Val said, "Let's walk home before we ministrate," and I begged my mother, who scrunched up her mouth, then gave in. She drove off with The Gnome, waving, calling, "No puddles." I clicked my tongue and walked off with ten other girls down Unqua Road. We splashed through every puddle we came to. We sang "Yellow Submarine" so loudly lights snapped on in the houses we passed. It was fun for a while to pretend that I was one of them: a hip Age of Aquarius chick in a fluorescent poncho and vinyl boots, even if I lacked the poncho and boots. As we reached Merrick Road, Val stopped singing to say that she would never get a period. Two other girls said "Yeah," and I nodded. It didn't seem there in the rain to have very much to do with me either. I saw my mother waiting across Merrick Road with an umbrella and ran to her.

Most of the Unqua School, class of '70, was scheduled to transfer to Dulles Junior High, a faded gray-and-yellow building that looked more like a storage hangar for snowplows and park equipment. It was located, it went without saying, on the far side of Sunrise. It looked dangerous.

In Personal Health classes that fall students were drawing detailed diagrams of the plant *Cannabis sativa*—it was apparently everywhere, possibly in our own backyards, and we were to watch for it at all times. In Social Studies, in Study Hall, we saw films about it and other drugs, each consisting of the same three elements reshuffled: an avalanche of colorful pills; a scene in which a kid who seems drunk makes his way down a hall; background voices that chant "Bennies, dexies, reds." The pieces came together each time as the kid in the hall opened a bathroom door and walked—satanic voices now louder—to the mirror. Suddenly we'd hear a piercing scream, then discover, as the camera moved in for the closeup, that the boy's face had melted! (returning to normal after he'd exclaimed, "Phhhew. I'll never toke that cannabis stuff again").

On every mosaic-tiled staircase you heard confused whisperings about this cannabis, about The Beatles breaking up and about older girls, with breasts and black arm bands, who had thrown themselves down flights of stairs because of one or the other. In the nurse's office, at my grandparents', I studied *Life* magazine articles with titles like "Richie, Portrait of a Teenage Addict" that had the kid's yearbook photo next to a shot of the father at the funeral and a caption that read "What Went Wrong?" Beneath life as it was lurked the traces of disturbing change.

On Halloween a rumor passed back through cafeteria rows about girls who were supposedly pregnant—tough girls from blue-collar families who claimed never to remove gum from their mouths. Their situation was difficult to picture. Although I had some understanding of the mechanics involved, I could not imagine a girl my age—not even a girl from the identical houses near Dulles—ending up this way. Nor could I imagine her "doing something to get rid of it," as I'd heard one girl say. I had no idea what in the world that might be.

On Thanksgiving I was wrestling outside with Dennis and Randy from next door, vaguely pretending they were my boyfriends, when one of them said, "Hey, ugly, you're bleeding." I ran home and in my underwear discovered a dark red smear like a Jewish great-aunt's lipstick on a tissue. Sitting, stunned, on the toilet, I heard the soft, knowing voice of Karen Carpenter drip from a transistor radio in my room. She was singing "We've Only Just Begun," and with blood caked beneath my fingernails, I ran out to kick the radio across the floor. After reassembling it, I paced. How could I tell my mother? She might tell my father, or my sisters, who just the day before had laughed at my nipples, puffed up suddenly like two lips shaping a kiss. I certainly could not tell Val, who had not had her period, who had, as she'd hoped, remained flat. I decided not to mention it, ever, not even the next day when my mother winked and pointed to a blue drugstore box on my dresser.

Soon after, however, it was 1971. I was twelve, and though menstruation continued, I forgot about it much of the time, along with nearly everything else. In just a matter of weeks, it seemed, I had become like the stick girl from the movie — shaky with change, a plain little figure about to come colorfully to life.

In February Gwyn moved out of our room, arranging her 500 stuffed mice in a wagon, scraping off the stickers of feet making the peace sign to put up again in my father's office, which was moved, model airplanes and jars of india ink, across the playroom downstairs into the garage. I promptly ordered new paint — a shade of pink so hot it would glow in the dark — and to go with it, a poster of the Black Power fist. I would lie awake all night staring at my fist, then in morning wander out across the lawn, forgetting to take my lunch or to kiss my mother. At school, cutting past a crowd of popular kids by the central stairs, I'd forget where exactly homeroom was in relation to my locker. Returning home in afternoon, I'd find that the house had shrunk considerably in my absence.

By March the house was the size of a dresser drawer. Or possibly, I thought, the world outside had expanded, closed in on me and my room the way a person in a game of red light, green light gets surprisingly closer, bigger somehow each time you turn around. I overheard my mother laugh into her hand and use the phrase "hormonal haze" in front of my father, who replied, "Let us hope." The stair crowd at school seemed to grow thicker.

By May I walked whenever possible with my eyes closed, hoping that I might more intensely experience the senses of smell and touch, or at least be surprised when I finally looked. One day I peeked to find myself at the edge of the staircase crowd. Girls in short leather skirts were pretending to faint. As they dropped, I saw beyond them to a group of boys by the wall, the gang's long-haired, leather-banded nucleus. They wore jeans that gathered in a ripply V at the crotch. Precisely angled bangs sliced their faces so that you saw one eye only.

I stared at them. Val, who unbelievably had put some socks inside a bathing suit top she called a bra, nudged me and said, "I'm getting out of here, let's go." I was about to follow when one bang boy looked straight at me and pointed. Two others started pointing, and then the first one winked at me and all three whistled—the two-toned approval I had heard applied to other girls. Val said, "Jesus, gross," and pulled me off. I was too shocked to speak, vindicated with these two notes after a lifetime of "See ya later, Ju-dy" as the entire class left early for catechism. I walked with Val a few feet, got picked up by a crowd near General Science and floated off without saying goodbye.

The last day of school that year, I stole two cigarettes from my father and walked with Val—who said, "Since when are you so cool?"—to the nearby community pools. While Val practiced cannonball dives off the low board, I looked out across the water to a crowd: the girls from the stairwell with some tough gum girls, none of them really pregnant, all, in fact, wearing bikinis and leather waist bracelets from the Stop Shop, the black-lighted boutique on Merrick Road I had been forbidden to enter. I moved my towel closer and then closer, and was only a few feet away when a subsection of bang boys came swooping onto the pool grounds—popping wheelies, lighting cigarettes with one hand and inhaling.

There were four whose names I knew: Billy "Boat" Brody, Jason Donohue, Kenny Puglia from General Science lab and some kid they called Bambie. With the studied moves of a motorcycle gang they dropped their bikes, unrolled cigarette packs from white T-shirt sleeves and threw a few girls into the deep end, screaming, "Rag." I watched them haul one "rag" girl out and hold her down, Boat Brody gripping her shoulders, Ken Puglia squatting on her feet while the kid named Bambie slapped her stomach—the sex "base" roughly between second and third that boys referred to as "pink belly." From the bus I had watched boys give out pink bellies at the side of the school. I had watched other girls stand by, watching their feet, just as they pretended not to notice the "rag" girl in front of me now. The girl finally escaped on her own and Boat and Bambie chased her. Ken Puglia, who seemed to possess a single, thick eyebrow resembling a headband, got up, looked around and walked over to stand at my feet. He demanded a cigarette. Silently, I handed him the two that I'd stolen and felt my own stomach burn, which I interpreted as my life changing, forever.

That night I moved the handmade stuffed animals into the closet—checking from time to time to be sure none were suffocating—and thought of Jason Donohue, the smallest, most cuddly of the boys. Like the others, Jason had grown his bang to proper length, but it hung in his right eye like a piece of wayward plant. He wore the standard white T-shirt, only his clung reassuringly to a roll of fat. The next day I stared directly at him, and Jason, his eyes a bleached egg-blue, his black hair soft and floppy as a 1965 Beatle's, stared back. Several hours later he approached my towel. After stammering a minute, he said, "Buy you french fries?"

Eating my french fries five at once, I watched Boat Brody, a tall, sweet-faced boy popular with girls, kick the bark off a tree. Jason put his arm around me and said, "Don't pay any attention to Mr. Romeo. He's just jealous that I got you. I think he felt like going out with a smart girl." This amounted to more male attention in ten minutes than I'd had in twelve years. I closed my eyes, attempting to review the past two days. When I opened them seconds later, Boat, so named for his shoe size, had carved out a bald spot on his tree. Jason had moved his hand from my shoulder onto my breast. Trying to loose a french fry stuck on my thong, I said, "I have to set the table," smiled, and ran off in the direction of my house.

My father, as I reached Moccasin Lane, was whistling us in for dinner. Remembering that my life had changed forever, I nearly panicked. But thinking quickly, I knew: I'd simply lead a double life! The boys could go home to their brick houses and beer; I'd go back to the Barrère nocturne I was preparing with Gwyn for recital. I raced up to the house behind my sisters, my father patting our heads and counting —one, two, three—as we raced into the kitchen. My mother called from the playroom downstairs, "Wash your hands."

By July Val seemed to have decided not to go out—ever— unless it was with her mother to shop at Mays. Although it was hard to admit, this did not bother me one bit. I had begun to feel about Val as I did about my parents: I loved them, but being from the past, they would not understand the present; they would not, under any circumstances, believe that I was a girl for whom popular boys abused trees. Besides,

I told myself, there were other girls to hang around with.

One day a very tall, flat-chested girl I'd seen sulking at the fringes of the staircase crowd sat down on the edge of my towel. She smiled at me, revealing a dense network of braces, and announced that her name was Carolynne Ann Carroway —Caro for short, or "Caro-whack," which was what her brother, who was twenty, liked to call her. She lived one canal over from me in a run-down Cape Cod house with this brother, two parents who fought, four cats, a dog and several actressy blond sisters whose names began with C—Colleen, Connie, Cathleen—all of whom, Caro assured me, had seen the Beatles at Shea Stadium.

Caro had inherited from her siblings pairs of worn water buffalo sandals and, it was clear, a well-developed sense of cool. She kept her thin, dirty-blond hair strapped into a ponytail that stuck out above one ear like a faucet—the side-swept style being best, she'd explain, for concealing dark roots at the part. She knew how to blow perfectly constructed smoke rings, how to steal cigarettes from delis, and tended to hang carefully back in a crowd, yielding to those who were louder. I tried, as a result, to get her alone whenever possible.

With Caro I could perform: doing cartwheels, turning to blow out smoke so she'd think I inhaled, saying things like, "Jason, oh, and my parents are so *mean* to me—pigs!—and my older brother, who used to ride me on his bike, you know, my cross would get all twisty in the spokes, but he died in Vietnam, MIA, I mean, no not really, I mean. I'm just so. I don't know."

One July day Caro interrupted me and said, "Pretend you see your mother coming and take a drag off the cig." I did, and she said, "Now, gasp—'Haah, my mother's coming,'" and I did and then choked. Caro slapped me on the back. "Now you know how to inhale," she said, flipping

the ponytail from left ear to right. From that day on we
were best friends.

We spent the days of our twelfth summer looking for
Jason, or any boy, exploring the farthest outposts of the Massapequa wilderness—the parks and playgrounds way up by
Dulles, the gullies and ridges of the pit, a vast, empty hole
like a bomb crater on the far side of Sunrise. There were
hundreds of girls out on the hunt around town, eye-shadowed
nomads who'd stop to report sightings, perhaps boys down by
a canal or at a pot party behind some dark and distant house.
"Cool," we'd say, and we'd push on, waiting for something to
happen, riding every hour in the meantime past the new
clock at White's, praying the digital dots would not say 5:55,
when, under threat of losing my phone rights, I was to be
home.

My parents, by late July, had noticed a change. My mother
seemed to be constantly in my room, putting away laundry,
offering to brush the back of my hair, which I most often
missed. Inhaling sharply, she'd ask, "What have you been up
to?" or "Where's old Val these days?" and I'd reply, "Nothing,
I don't know, Caro's mother doesn't care where she is, Jesus."
My father, for his part, demanded that he answer the phone.
"Yes, young man," he would say, "my daughter Betsy is here,
you are correct in that. Yes, I am sure that you could, that
you are, we will assume, physiologically capable of speaking."
The boy would hang up and my father would shout, "Cretin,"
forcing me to shout, "Police state"—a term I had learned
from Caro—and my mother, acting quickly, to intervene.

But by August I had no time for my parents. I was concerned only with getting outside, as if I were propelled by a
physical force out the door and into streets I had previously

seen only from the backseat of our car. If on a given day nothing new or dramatic happened, I would invent some kind of drama—I might put eyeliner on Gwyn or show her how to clip the lit part of a cigarette so that you could relight it later. I decided one day to abandon the bra I'd begged for six months before. The day after, just to change, I broke up with Jason, explaining, as I'd heard Patty Duke explain on a made-for-TV movie, "I have to be free."

My first day of freedom, Boat Brody invited me to be the lone girl at a party in Ken Puglia's "hippie shack," one of the basement black-light poster rooms that boys my age had inherited from their brothers. I felt pretty, dressed in a white tank top and a pair of red shorts that came from Mays. I felt free, which is what I said to myself—You are free and pretty —as boldly I lay down in the shack to kiss Boat and Ken and some others. When they started pulling on my top I tried saying, It's a new experience! When I'd quickly had enough of this experience, I tried to get up. Ken Puglia, looking that day like Ape Number Five on the science chart of evolution, held back my shoulder. Boat, the dimples in his cheeks like two bullet holes, squeezed both my breasts with one hand.

When I returned home that afternoon my mother stopped vacuuming and said, "What happened? You look upset." I said, "Nothing happened. We played spin the bottle, kidding around," and ran upstairs to my room. When my hands stopped shaking I made a list of what I had learned about the sex experience since entering the real world in June:

1. Sex, I wrote, had something to do with "sperms," microorganisms like blood cells, only shaped like and roughly the same size as tadpoles.
2. Sperms were produced in the test tubes, two individual lumps of skin that hung at the side of a man's penis, still often referred to as his weenie or wiener, which

could, under certain conditions, change sizes.

3. Sperms were always leaking out and could live on their own for up to one year, meaning that . . .

4. Some problem, like pregnancy, could occur simply from a sperm landing on your clothes and finding its way inside months later, meaning that you ran to *wash immediately.*

5. Sperms were strengthened by heat. People tended to "do it" in the dark so that the sperm would remain cool.

6. If you put the penis only halfway in, the sperms would somehow be blocked and thus . . .

7. Sperms were a lot like menstrual blood: Each flowed back and forth. If you went into the water while you had your period, as everyone knew, the blood could be forced back up into the body, causing between five and seven internal organs to explode. This explained why boys were so eager to throw girls with their periods into water. It was, like the pink belly, a form of torture, an act of war.

The last week of the summer of 1971, I discovered others.

It had been a typical enough day at the pools. Boys stood in circles off to one side playing "Jimi Hendrix eats guitar"; girls stood in satellite groups, applying liquid foundation to look better tanned. At noon the two groups merged and walked to a pool party inside the Shores near my house. Caro skipped ahead to greet the hostess. I tried to follow, but someone grasped my shoulder, put a hand over my mouth and pulled me across the street to the Nassau Shores canal, where an old red barge was slowly sinking. Boat, who had grabbed me, held my arms. Ken Puglia tore the striped shirt my mother had bought me at the Stop Shop for the first day of school. The kid called Bambie pulled the top off a Magic Marker.

From the backyard across the way came faint splashing sounds and shrieks, like sound-track noise meant to indicate "kids/summer fun." The barge creaked. A woman got into a tan station wagon. But no one noticed me or came to help, and I froze, the way girls receiving pink bellies always froze, all time reduced to one moment: that afternoon, a bunch of boys holding me down as one of them wrote the word "slut" across my breasts, now the soft pointy shape of anthills.

They slapped hands in the air when they were through, got on their Stingrays and rode off. To my relief, Boat Brody pedaled back, arched high in a wheelie. He leaned his face close to mine for a kiss, I thought, for an apology, and then spit.

Jason walked out from the yard one minute later, glanced at the spit and then at Boat, who was halfway down the block. Without saying a word he climbed onto a new orange Stingray and pushed off. Something caught and flapped against his spokes as he rode. Watching him disappear, I heard the clacking noise of a projector as the film distorts and blurs and the lights come up to a roomful of groans.

The word had faded by Labor Day, but the boys never called to apologize. I was back more or less where I'd started —on a picnic with my family at the beach. Our father was taking our picture, telling us to hold still; our mother called, "Come on, ladies, smile." I put aside Anne Frank's *Diary of a Young Girl* and pictured myself anywhere else: in my mother's old red-carpeted apartment; on my way by plane to England; riding out of town toward the city on a Stingray, racing the train, high on pot so that I could not make out where I was going.

At midnight on September 8, my thirteenth birthday, I sat in the black beanbag chair I'd received as a gift. In my lap was a notebook my father had used for a biology course at

Brooklyn College in the forties. The paper was so old it smelled of slightly burned cardboard, of the ancient autumns preserved in Val's basement orkneys. I called my new diary "Dear Best Friend" and at the top of the first page wrote:

I am not anywhere as far as I can see.

T W O

In 1971 all life in the eighth grade flowed from a battered Baggie containing:

—eye shadow (liquid, green)
—eyeliner to finesse the neo-Cleopatra swirl, the oriental lower lid

—white foundation to ensure a face with the quality of chalk
—frosted white lip gloss to match it

It went without saying that your eyebrows were now the width of bobby pins. If you'd done a careful job, then, you emerged from your bag looking distant, like a mysterious sylph so pale there were surely secrets, a possible bruise or two beneath. This appealingly slutty look, based in the dark-linered eyes and ghostly lips of sixties *Vogue,* seemed to fuse naturally with the hippie sartorial style and the mien of a suburban punk. Caro Carroway called the effect "nonchalant," named for the way she'd casually case a store she planned to shoplift, reducing herself to a thin sliver, to a girl who was there but not there.

Nonchalance to me seemed a significant social movement on a par roughly with that of beatniks or hippies. Quickly I made a study of my sad, slouching peers to conclude that *(a)* the true nonchalant was, like Caro, a girl with older siblings who'd at least once been busted, pregnant, drafted or arrested, and that *(b)* nonchalance, as an attitude, as a necessary life choice, was concentrated among girls of the more popular social classes, girls who, to be cool, would do whatever necessary to emulate these older siblings. I was not, therefore, an obvious candidate.

Still, dressing in stark, ratty black and white, standing with all weight thrown on one hip and using key phrases ("Get off my case, Mother"; "What do you *want* from my life?") seemed a natural extension of the poses and events of the summer before. It was, more to the point, like belonging to a club at last and, even better, to a movement! I decided to act nonchalant.

I sat on a curb outside school each morning watching girls who claimed to be named Desiderata or Déjà Vu smoke cigarettes down to the filter, then fall over, choking, onto friends. I roamed from Dulles back to the Shores each afternoon, smoking dejectedly in parking lots, in the Mays bathroom by Lingerie, any place out in the world that had no carpet. I imagined myself as Déjà Vu, a girl who fainted regularly and greeted her friends by shrieking, "Doll, how ya fuckin' doin'?" As it happened, I'd remain quietly off to one side watching Caro, who seemed unconsciously to park herself at crowd's center. Then I'd go home to do schoolwork.

One day, out grazing in a parking lot, we met Déjà Vu—in real life, Hilaree Crane, a very white, emaciated girl with a gold peroxide streak through black waist-length hair and, she said, an actual checking account tied to her parents'. Next she said, "I ran into my mother, the rich bitch, in Food Fair. She didn't fucking recognize me. I went home and ate half a jar of Vaseline, you know, to kill myself. I threw up. I covered my body with the rest and lit a match. I wrote a song called 'I Am a Naked Candle on My Bed.' Then I threw up."

I stared at her, trying to determine whether or not she was kidding. I thought of my mother, of Val, and missed them both. Caro, on the other hand, nodded. "So," she asked, "did your mother notice you were, you know, like waxy?" And they began to talk about their mothers and their older sisters and Caro's father, who thought her name was Karen. I tried to join the conversation. I said, "Right fucking on." Caro, flipping her ponytail, said, "Huh?" Hilaree, known for so complete a command of the oriental lid that boys called her "Mao," squinted one blackened eye and laughed.

In 1971 the Massapequa we had known as small children was about to vanish. Within three years, a vast two-tiered shopping mall would spring up on the site of the Sunrise pit. The Highway would be expanded and rerouted to service it;

the old shopping centers—White's, Mays and Bar Harbour
—would be closed, and many that fall had already hung out
colored banners to announce "The Final Days!" As nonchalants we haunted these landmarks, hoping to inspire the same
sad effects produced by listening, hours on end, to the most
badly scratched old Beatle records we could find.

Bar Harbour, one of the original outdoor shopping centers,
faced the earliest demise. Food Fair—my first words of English—had tied together its shopping carts in one long,
swaying row that looked, from a distance, like a mutant silver
Slinky. Caro and I climbed onto it one Saturday to watch
workmen remove the pink neon sign that said Kresge's. Hilaree later on found the blue *e* in Gimbels, laid it across a cart
and rolled it home. Those were the highlights. Most afternoons, slightly bored, we'd wander off down Merrick toward
Nassau Shores, the county line and Amityville—site of the
slowly sinking barge, Hardee's hamburgers and, it was
hoped, of "depression," a new condition Hilaree and Caro had
heard about from their sisters.

I would personally do everything in my power to act depressed. I'd walk along wincing as if suffering from headache.
In Hardee's, playing "Pass the ice from straw to straw," I'd
contract my muscles, then sigh as I released them, hoping
others might think me weak with despair. My effort was
helped along most Saturdays by actual boredom, by the way
the hours limped, measured in spilled salt and ashes, the torn
ketchup packs on the table, by the way you eventually ate
ketchup straight and didn't care.

Back at home, my parents would come into my room and
start talking.

"Sweetheart," my mother would begin, "did you and the
girls have a nice day?"

"What is that smoky smell?" my father would say. "Have
you been near a fire? Have you practiced your flute today?" to

be interrupted by my mother asking, "Are you all right? You look mopey," until both were tripping on words and questions, drawing Gwyn and Sashi to my room as if to the scene of an accident. Realizing that I'd eaten nothing but ketchup, I'd say, "I am just hungry. Get off my case, do you mind?"

My sisters would whisper, "What's wrong with her?" and my mother, pulling my frowning father by a cuff from the room, would explain, "She's just thirteen years old, that's what's wrong. Now give her breathing room, come on."

Soon every girl I knew was officially depressed. For a while it had seemed that they, like me, were only faking—rehearsing desperation as diligently as they practiced with mascara, showing it off as they might have a peace-sign patch on their pants. But by mid-fall it had become clear that junior high school mass-produced this feeling.

In the Dulles principal's office there was a large color portrait of Richard Nixon and, beneath it, an ex-marine who sat all day issuing memos about student unrest. As it applied to the eighth grade, this meant that all girls baring shoulder or thigh were to be sent home for "suitably conservative attire." Those late for class or otherwise arousing suspicion were to be interrogated: Where had they been? With whom? Had they been offered marijuana, downs, uppers, bennies, reds? Unless she was looking to be questioned about "hard narcotics," the girl with an oriental eyelid walked quickly through the halls with her mysteriously pale face discreetly down. I preferred to walk this way myself. As the fall progressed, I had to look up for one thing alone: to see if I had landed near Boat, who was sure to break down and apologize.

Three months had passed since early summer, since the time I'd been a popular, cute girl boys were in love with.

Now the boys I'd known had disappeared. They had, I was afraid, become The Past. I mentioned this strange and sorry loss of time one day to my friends. Caro slammed her locker, looked at Hilaree and then at me as if I'd embarrassed her. "What are you talking about?" she said. "It's only last month."

That afternoon Boat Brody turned up at last, glaring down at me outside Home Ec, biceps straining against a faded blue work shirt, one deep dimple pinching his cheek as he sneered. Trying to seem casual, I said, "Oh, hi." Boat, as if playing quarterback, rammed my shoulder, snorted, then walked off. I turned to follow, to ask if perhaps he had me confused with someone else, but he had raised his third finger high into the air. He called out, "Slut."

I sat shaking for a while in a bathroom, then emerged to find classes underway. Based on the rooms and the angle of the stairwell, I could not say for sure where I was. As I stood trying to retrace my steps, a thick hand landed on my shoulder. It was a teacher this time, his teeth clamped as if his jaw were wired shut.

"Okay, missie," he spit, "let's have it and no crap. What is it? Dexies? Downers?" Thinking quickly, I explained that I'd gotten "my friend" and that I'd been, uh, unprepared. Red dots the size of radishes appeared on the teacher's cheeks. He pulled a dime from his pocket. "Here," he mumbled, "get yourself fixed up, but don't let me catch you doing this again." Walking away, I realized that I had for the first time lied to a teacher. Boat had not apologized. I became, that day, officially depressed.

By late October depression as a topic had been supplanted by sex. Everyone I knew was obsessed with it. Not that anyone directly said so. Embarrassed, without essential facts, even the most supremely nonchalant approached the subject through dramatic device.

There was, for instance, the popular practice of hyperventilating—breathing in short little gasps as someone, usually Caro, wrapped a belt around your neck, causing you to fall, as realistically as you could, moaning, "Fuck me." There was to accompany it the apocalyptic sex rumor hinting most often at the miseries of pregnancy, something far more likely to occur now, it was agreed, than in the times of the bouffant girls who'd screamed at Beatles.

A few days before Halloween, sitting outside the Shore East Diner on Merrick Road, Hilaree choked Caro, then shrieked, "I know someone who did it!"

"Did what?" I asked, pulling Caro's ponytail to be sure she was still breathing. "You mean the real 'It'?"

Hilaree winked and said, "No, I mean what you do if—if you get pregnant. You have to kick it! My sister Darlena kicked someone's stomach right in the Shore East bathroom."

I had by now grasped certain facts: how and when one might become pregnant, how long it could be expected to last. This, however, was news. I watched my feet, unsure of what to say. Caro sat up, rubbing her neck. Hilaree, displeased with our response, shouted, "Ingrates," and walked off.

"What bullshit," Caro said, sounding as if she'd inhaled helium. "Hilaree's sister didn't *do* it, she *had* it kicked, just like my sister had it a different way." I wondered if, like a better stereo, this was something every older sister had. But Caro was talking. "You don't really *kick* it anyway," she said, "you drink rubbing alcohol. Or, you know, there are just girls who disappear. They have it someplace and one day they're gone. You never really see them again."

"So where do they go?" I asked as we walked back through the Shores.

"You never find out," she said with a shrug. "Some girls just fall that way. That's the dice."

If the air was heavy with rumors of sex and disaster, it was clouded too with talk of drugs. I had, by November, seen something of these fabled drugs: thin cigarettes tucked in bathroom Baggies, guys snoring in Study Hall, girls in Gym so stoned they could not cross to the left during a folk dance of the Balkans. Then one day, as had been prophesied by Health class films, a voice behind me whispered, "The boys have Colombo weed."

I turned to find Caro and Hilaree. Caro said, "They get it from these new ninth-grade guys—Jim Scabb and Steven Bono, whose brothers are friends with their brothers—and they carry it in makeup Baggies to the White's parking lot at night." Hilaree said, "I think we should go. I haven't gotten high in days."

Aside from inhaling lit catnip, Hilaree, like Caro and me, had never gotten high in her life. But if we did, I thought, I might see at last what had gone wrong, how it was that boys who had loved me could ever write such a word across my chest. I said okay.

After a decade, Friday night arrived. Finishing dinner in two minutes, thirty seconds, I excused myself to paint on my features, then maneuvered craftily back past the kitchen. I was almost out the door when my father shouted, "Whoa!"

I took a step back. "Yes, Dad?"

"Young lady," he said, turning in his chair. "Where exactly are you going with that crap on your face?"

I said, "I'm going to a dance," and Gwyn said, "She's going

to see Boat, Boatie, Boat," inciting Sashi to chant, "Boot, boot," so that my mother had to say, "Girls, please." My father said, "All right. But you are to be back in this house at 9:15 — not a second later."

"Ma," I whined, "he's wrecking my whole life." My mother touched his hand and said, "Honey, I don't see the harm," but my father was getting up. I opened the door. I shouted, "You can't come where I'm going," and ran across the lawn, the sounds of dinner, my father's shouts, fading cinematically behind me. By the time Caro, Hilaree and I had reached the White's parking lot — a paved square extending from Sunrise down to Unqua School and across to the Tremor High School field — I had revised this dinner scene to include death threats and tossed knives. I had become a revolutionary. Confidently, I looked around.

About fifty kids stood in small clumps, while the new boys who had pot stood in a circle off to one side. We eased into a group. Then, just as I'd pictured it, the joint came. Imitating other girls, I pinched it with two fingers and made a sucking noise that sounded like *shoe*. The papery smoke burned my throat as if I'd run an emery board over it, but like the others, I bravely made a sound like *heep* and held it in.

As Caro had warned, boys were patrolling the circles, checking to be sure that no one — especially not some "chick" — was wasting their dope. Girls, as I could have predicted, were pretending to faint. When Ken Puglia, the eyebrow now thick as a whisk broom, passed on watch, Hilaree fell conveniently at his feet. Pushing me aside, Ken scooped her up and carried her off toward the fence that ran between White's and the high school. I wondered if this had really happened or if I was simply stoned. I glanced at Caro for her reading. Caro, standing hopefully beside the muscular red-haired boy named Jim Scabb, watched the top of Hilaree's head disappear down a slope, and then shrugged. I looked once more at the stream, at Caro, then turned back to find Boat Brody parked at my side. His eyes were puffy as if with poison ivy. He seemed taller. "You," he said with a burp, "let's go for a walk."

Assuming that I was indeed high, I followed him to the stream bank, where we lay bathed in the yellowish, drizzly haze cast by parking-lot lights. I felt romantic. Boat looked at me, focused, and ripped open the snaps of my new fringed suede coat. From somewhere down the stream, Hilaree giggled. I thought of my parents having dinner. I said, "Can I go now?" Boat put a hand over my face in response. He shoved the other hand down my pants and, when I squirmed, inserted his third finger inside me.

At 9:16, ten minutes after Boat had at last removed his finger, I lay panting in the beanbag. "Look," my mother was saying, "you know that Daddy has a short temper, and there's been a lot of change lately. But if it's just—and I'll take your word for this, Betsy—dances *with* chaperones, and if you get home on time, then we shouldn't have these problems. Now don't go to sleep with that mascara on, as we discussed, sweetie, promise?" I nodded, kissed her and got undressed striptease-style in front of the mirror. On one breast I noticed a red blotch like a bug bite. I determined that it was a hickey and, as Hilaree had advised on the run home, took a hairbrush in hand to scrape it off.

The following Monday Caro informed me that Hilaree, over the weekend, had tried to kill herself. "Ken said Hils had no tits," she reported, "so Hils ate half a tube of Ben-Gay."

My mind raced: I was shocked; I was jealous of Caro, who knew instead of me; I was thinking for some reason about my mother. I imagined saying, "Mom, it's Hilaree. She ate Ben-

Gay," and the way she would stare at me in horror. I imagined telling her anything else about my new teen life and provoking a similar response.

At lunch the next day Hilaree reappeared wearing a white neck brace she'd decorated with felt doves that looked like loaves of bread. While searching the medicine cabinet, she had apparently had an idea. "We should carve boys' names into our arms," she wheezed, one hand to her neck, "you know, like with razors. It's cheaper than getting tattoos." I walked out of the cafeteria, attempting to determine how things had gotten to this point, connecting in my mind a happy childhood with nonchalance, the "slut" word, Ben-Gay and now razors! One thing seemed clear: I would have to close the gap between the person I'd always been and the one I sort of was now. The way to do it, I decided, would be to make Boat—symbol of all that had gone wrong—love me as he had before things happened.

I walked that afternoon down to Caro's, where I found my two friends on a bed, sorting through used blades. Caro said that she planned to carve *JS* for Jim Scabb, though all he'd said so far was, "Carol, you gotta match?" Hilaree planned to etch *KP* for Kenny Puglia, while I was going to write out *Boat*. Sitting against the door, Caro tentatively scratched her *J*. Hilaree chickened out and sat in a corner French-inhaling a Salem, while I closed my eyes and let the razor lightly run across the flesh.

The following day some guys who knew Hilaree grabbed my arm and pulled me to the attendance office, where Boat was sitting out a solitary detention. Moving his lips, Boat Brody read the scratchy pink lines. "Shee-it," he exclaimed when he'd finished, "and I hate her guts." The boys laughed and took turns examining my arm until, in tears, I broke away and ran to a bathroom. Above the toilet someone had written: *Boat Brody love Jilli Ann Piscataro—the Piss! She lie down for pink belly. She a nimpho!* Shaking, I crossed out Jilli Ann's name and filled in my own. I wrote the same thing on my desk the next period. Then I went home, claiming to be sick, and stayed in my room for a week.

When I went out again it was December. I began my days by wrapping rubber bands around my shirt cuffs to be sure no boy would see or laugh at my arm. Then, missing the bus, I would walk alone to school, imitating the monotone Hilaree spoke in to chant as I'd tell myself, Nothing really has changed in my life. By late December, when I could at last stop cutting off circulation at the wrist, I nearly believed it. Winter Festival, as proof, arrived as usual.

Winter Festival eve, Gwyn stopped in my room to use the full-length mirror we had once shared. She looked me up and down. "You're wearing that?" she said.

"What?" I said, annoyed. "What's wrong with it?"

"It's so short it looks like a shirt and not a dress."

"Shut up, Gwyn," I replied.

"I can't wait to hear what Aunt Ruth says," Gwyn giggled, combing her hair back into barrettes.

"Shut up, Gwyn," I said again, and walked downstairs ahead of her to greet the fake-relatives, who had gathered in the living room, a blur of foil-covered bowls and violins brought for carols.

We started with fake-Uncle Benny. Benny flashed his JFK tennis-star smile, said "So?" and then "Great," which was all he would say until next year. Behind him was fake-Aunt Ruth. She grabbed Gwyn's face and in a high, excited voice said, "Report!" I watched her Maybelline mouth open and close, the subtly shaded Suzy Parker eyebrows arching. As a child I had loved Aunt Ruth, loved leaning against her shoulder at the piano, staring deep into the heart of her corsage. Now I smiled in dread. After the kiss she stood back, folded her hands and said, "I hear from your guidance counselor that you're not doing A work this term."

"So I got two B's and one bad mark in Home Ec. So what?"

She lifted the eyebrows into perfect boomerangs. I turned to greet my fake-cousins—Donnie, a prizewinning trumpet player, who seemed always to keep his lips in the mouthpiece shape, and Lisette, an artist, who worked with brown clay. Both regularly traveled on Jewish youth outings to places like Israel, sending postcards fake-Aunt Ruth supplemented with slide-show presentations. We all attended the same schools, but our fake-cousins seemed to us like foreigners, and we liked to pretend at Winter Festival that Lisette was French, that we would in the morning be going on a plane with her to Paris.

From across the room I heard Aunt Ruth ask, "What is that guck on her face?" and my mother say, "Now, now. Come on." I said, to no one in particular, "I'll go sort decorations," and ran down the stairs to the playroom. Aunt Ruth followed.

"I hear you've dropped ballet," she whispered, fondling a tiny china acorn.

Arranging the skirt on a paper angel, I said, "It's boring just to stand there—"

"Donnie," she interrupted, "has been accepted by the Long Island Youth Orchestra. They'll be touring Japan and the Philippines. If your playing was in shape, we might have considered you. But I've heard you've slid downhill. It's the year," she said, stopping to kiss Sashi, who'd brought her a cookie, "when the nonachievers are weeded out." I walked into the bathroom and slammed the door. When I opened it Aunt Ruth was waiting. "I think your mascara's running," she said.

It was freezing on the side stoop, but I did not care. I was

not going to sit inside with these people. A while later my
mother came out and stood above me, the sounds of "Hark!
The Herald Angels Sing" and my father's anxious voice rising
behind us.

"What is this on your favorite night? You wait for this all
year. What are you doing out here freezing?"

I had no idea what to tell her. I figured I'd better stick
with the immediate. I said, "I hate Aunt Ruth."

"Honey, Ruth is just concerned."

"She's a bitch, Mommy."

"Now come on. I don't want to hear you use that language."

"This is the worst Winter Festival of my life," I said,
bursting into tears.

"Come on, my big girl," she said, kneeling at my side in
the snow. "No tears. Now we'll finish decorating the tree.
And then there's the final tree lighting and the cookies you
girls did such a lovely job on. Granddaddy will read 'Twas
The Night Before Christmas, and then. . . ." Her voice was
headed up the scale, and by the time she'd said "a much-
needed day of rest," she was practically singing. I let her hug
me and walked with her back inside.

Caro came by after Christmas with a present—a red candle
in the shape of a heart. Lighting it, inhaling the match
fumes, she stared solemnly out across the flame. "Okay," she
said, "so Boat is a jerk. Forget it! Steve Bono—Jim Scabb's
bestest friend, just like I'm your best friend—is having a
New Year's Eve party."

Steve, she informed me, was the younger brother of the
fabulous Mickey Bono, Tremor senior and secret leader of the
Pit Boys gang who wore the dragon costume at football
games and danced with cheerleaders. I had seen Mickey Bono

as the dragon, and he was actually cute. I had been on the same page of *The Hobbit* for three days. "Okay," I told her, "I'll try to come."

On New Year's Eve Steven Bono held open his screen door and said, "Why, it's little Busty and long tall Caro-line." He picked us up and carried us into a tiny foyer, past a paint-by-number Jesus, past a closet and into the light. It was the first time I had seen one of the older ninth-grade boys up close.

Like Mickey, Steve was short and stocky. He had dimples like Mickey, and like Mickey, arms so twisted with muscles it looked as if he'd shoved a loaf of Friday-night challah beneath his sleeves. Steve also had the weirdest hair I'd ever seen. It was nearly white, as if he were an albino with eye color, and strangely cut—wavy parted bangs on a level with the eyebrows, the rest straight down the back in a wispy ponytail.

"Party time, children," Steve said. He put us down, took my fringed suede coat and pointed to the basement stairs.

There were kids everywhere—on the arms of furniture, on line to get inside Mickey's hippie shack far at the back of the room. Hilaree lay with Ken Puglia on a pool table. Boat, wearing a white sweater, balanced some girl on his lap. Noticing me, he brushed the girl aside as if dismissing a cat that was shedding. I turned to face a wall. I pretended to study the wallpaper—a confused green-and-white tableau depicting life in ancient Pompeii. There was "Feast Day," "Debate in the Senate," "Peasants Doing Laundry at the Forum." I felt as if I'd been there before, then realized that Val's parents had this paper in their bedroom, which reminded me that I had not called my old best friend, not even on Christmas. I picked up a beer, drank it too rapidly and sat down to smoke a joint with Jason.

"Jason," I said, wiping my nose on his white sweater. "Do you think Val is mad at me? Are you mad at me? I just messed everything up." Jason did not respond. Drinking half another beer, smoking from a hash pipe, I looked up to ask why and saw that it was not Jason I leaned on, but Boat. And we were moving, he was carrying me back into the hippie room, although I was stoned for the first time, drunk, and thus could not say for sure.

When I opened my eyes, Boat was sitting on my stomach and a loose, slimy strand, either saliva or a spider web, was inching its way toward my face. I concentrated on a velvety poster of a black girl tied to a motorcycle, her Afro blending with the smoke from a hookah held by some guy who looked like Christ. When I looked up again, Boat had placed his penis on my nose. He mumbled, "Suck it, you nympho." I might have tried, but other penises appeared at its side, bobbing and wagging so that I saw just a blur of beige Jell-O. I turned my head and called for Caro or Hilaree. I turned it the other way and smacked my cheek against a large wooden spool that held a candle. "Let go," I begged, tasting blood on my lip, and someone shouted, "Hold her down." I said, "Please stop." Boat moaned, "Suck it," saying it again and again until at last Steven Bono, pushing in the door, knocking Boat over, shouted, "Cut it. Get the fuck out of here— all of you." I stood, wobbled for a moment, then walked over to the couch where Caro and Hilaree sat, huge smiles like watermelon slices arranged on their faces. Hilaree giggled and tipped over. Caro burped and closed her eyes. I ran upstairs. Mickey Bono, one silent blonde at this side, appeared to drive me home.

I avoided my family when I got in, ran past Coco, the new dog, and went straight to my room. Hours or possibly minutes later I awoke, sensing the presence of vomit. My hair was wet. I put a hand on my pillow. It slid right off. Holding my desk lamp like a torch, I saw crusted speckles on my wall. My father, pushing open the door, noticed them too.

"Get out," I said, jumping up. "You have to knock."

"You listen to me," he said, coming toward me. "You lied to us, and I will not tolerate dishonesty. You said you'd be at a Miss Hilaree Crane's? Well, we called the Crane residence, attempting to wish you a happy New Year. The Cranes were entertaining on their own and knew of no such plans. They informed us that you were, in actuality, with a certain Bono family." He had backed me into a corner. Poking my chest with his index finger, he barked, "Who are these people?"

"I just went to a party," I said.

He slapped me. "You've been drinking. You stink of booze. Just look at yourself."

"I ate peanut butter," I sobbed. "The kind with the jelly stripes through it. It made me sick."

"This has gone too far," my father said, backing away. "Now, I've watched it coming and I've tried to be patient, to see it, out of respect for your mother, as a phase. But for Christ's sake, enough! It's a new year. Let's make a clean break. For starters, you're in the house—two weeks—to get your head screwed back on." And he walked out as my mother and sisters walked in with towels to help clean up.

On New Year's Day I looked in the mirror and noticed that my front tooth had cracked up one side, leaving a pointy spear that caught my tongue. I remembered hitting my head on the hippie spool and tasting blood. Trying to remain calm, I said out loud, "It just broke and then fell apart later." I thought about this for a minute, almost screamed, took several deep breaths and ran outside. Then I ran back in to say that I'd fallen. It was effective: My mother gasped and made an emergency dentist appointment. My father, forgiving me for the duration of the crisis, drove me over in silence.

I returned to find Hilaree and Caro in the beanbag chair.

"God," Hilaree squeaked, "what happened to your tooth?"

"Well, you know," I said calmly, "it's just one of the risks of a nonchalant."

Hilaree and Caro looked at each other and then at me. "What does that mean?" asked Hilaree.

"You know, nonchalants. How we are?"

"Come on, Betsy," said Caro, "it's just a word. It's not how we are."

"But it's like hippies," I said, the panic I'd delayed on the rise. "You know, like a club."

Caro snorted and said, "It is not. It's just like the way you stood, you know. What's that have to do with hippies? You imagine things more than any girl I know."

"Hippies are dead," Hilaree said, lying back in the bean-bag. "It's just girls out on their own now."

I sat there for a long time after they'd gone, beans running to the center of the chair, the tastes of blood and cement in my mouth, an ache in my tooth running straight up a nerve into my cheek. Outside on South Merrick Road some boy screamed, "Fuckin' 1972." It was a New Year.

I stayed in my room for the two weeks without leaving. I reread *Jane Eyre* because it would take a while. I ignored the way my mother called "All right in there?", lit the heart and wrote to my diary. When that grew dull I tried writing to the heart. *Dear Candle,* I wrote one afternoon, *I am here in my room.* I read this back to myself, picked up the heart and threw it at an early Beatle record I had played fifty times in one day.

Caro showed up again at the end of the second week. She brought with her a nickel bag of pot her cousin had left beneath her pillow as a wisdom-tooth gift. Hilaree, she told

me as we walked down Merrick Road, would be going to
Europe for Easter break, to Canada for the summer and then
to Massapequa High, the crosstown school. "Us Tremor High
girls have to stick together," Caro said, slipping an arm
through mine. I nodded and took the joint, the next one and
the one after, until I felt my head throb with the sound of
crickets far out in the country and could not hear a word that
Caro said.

This went on throughout the spring and summer of 1972.
One late July day, stoned on the park swings that crested
high out over Merrick Road, I at last arrived at a solution.
The answer to my problem—the cure for my loneliness, for
the atrocities of Boat—was obviously Jason: I would love
Jason, who had never been like the others, even if he had
grown his hair down to his waist.

And so Jason took me back, only to leave me soon after,
unswayed by the new halter top my mother had sewn from a
piece of real silk. He said, "You can't predict if you're gonna
like someone the next week." Caro, releasing her ponytail,
said, "At least you had a boyfriend for a little while." I fell
over in the beanbag chair and cried so hard I had to peel my
cheek from the vinyl. Still, life continued. I went to flute
lessons. I studied gymnastics, under the influence of Olga
Korbut, and went bowling with Caro and Denise Martin, a
fleshy, red-cheeked blonde I'd known in ballet who had
changed her name to Rainbo. I was no longer nonchalant,
although I was still very pale, officially depressed, definitely
nervous all the time. One day during the fall of 1972, our
Social Studies teacher, Miss Cella, tried to explain why.

The problem, she said, stabbing the map of Africa with a
rubber pointer, was that our generation was "inherently unin-
teresting." People ten years older, people born in 1948 like
her and her twin brother, Tony Cella: *They* were interesting.

Putting down the pointer, she folded her hands and said, "You are the detritus." If I hadn't been so tired, I would have looked up this word in the dictionary my parents had given me on my fourteenth birthday the week before. But the precise meaning didn't matter. It was the most plausible explanation for things I had heard.

T H R E E

By late 1972 marijuana had set-
tled in on Long Island like McDonald's: It was fast, it was
easy, it was everywhere.

For the girls of the Tremor ninth grade, it had filled the

void created by the decline of group fainting and play-suicide. As a newly turned fourteen-year-old, you retired your white lipstick and instead collected the paraphernalia of pot; specifically, you placed into a tiny leather bag that hung from a frayed knotted string at your waist:

—Bambu rolling papers you practiced licking, attempting to keep the saliva solely on the thin strip of glue
—tweezers known as roach clips, decorated with snakes and skulls and used to hold the ragged, burned-out tip of a joint
—Visine

The pot community at Tremor High—on any given day, some 60 percent of the 3,500-member student body—gathered in a wooded marsh area that extended from the parking lot a quarter mile down to Merrick Road. Members of the class of 1972, having won for us the right to roam unpoliced during free periods, had named the woods Zappaland (*Whose woods are these, Frank Zappa knows,* as it was scribbled on desks and bathroom stalls). By that fall "Zappa" had become the Grand Boulevard of Tremor, an updated version of the seventh-grade stair crowd or the street-corner sit-in outside Dulles in eighth. At 8:10 each morning, a mushroom cloud of dope ascended through its mossy trees, where it stuck—a dramatic bayou effect that throughout the day attracted a platoon of green-army-coated boys followed by girls in corduroy bell-bottoms, girls with stringy shag haircuts, girls wearing the new round-toed, clown-footed style of Earth Shoe.

Although I had gotten high on weekends, on summer days in the park, I had not yet officially been "zapped," not become one of the kids who stared obsessively at their desks during class, silently fingering a pencil, mouthing *wah.*

But one October night in my room, schoolbooks surrounding me in a fan, one triangle of cinnamon incense dwindling, I considered that my social life had been reduced, basically, to sobbing over Jason, which I interrupted Mondays for flute lessons. The next day, Caro and I ate lunch outside with Denise Martin, whose new "Rainbo" image required that she wear gauze drawstring dresses and that she smell at all times of lemon. We walked down the scuffed dirt path into Zappa, smoked five bowls of what Caro's cousin had described as "outrageous shit" and waited to feel the familiar tightness above the ears. Later I wandered out to French I and, feeling "into it," volunteered to translate three paragraphs of *Petit Pierre Lapin* in front of a class of fifty. It went surprisingly well. I got high before school, in Study Hall, before Gym, nearly every day thereafter.

My parents noticed a change almost immediately: Suddenly I *loved* school. I openly loved my father and my flute. I said, "Sure, I'll babysit Sashi." Being high, I had discovered, unlike being drunk, was something you could insert into everyday life, carry around with you like a diary stashed inside a leather purse. Experienced parents such as Caro's shrugged it off, considered it as integral to adolescence as hanging out. Parents like mine, new to this world, unfamiliar with the symptoms, never suspected. A girl that year could simply float through life—to the school, to the woods and home— in a new way, there but not there.

There were a few rules in the outdoor wing of Tremor. Fortunately they were simple.

Rule One: Boys had the pot and girls hung on to their arms, giggling, trying to get as much as they could. For this I soon found myself in an excellent position. As it grew colder, as the trees of Zappa slowly froze, Steven Bono— brother of the fabulous Mickey, possessor of only "righteous" weed—became my first official boyfriend.

It happened one night after Jason, shouting, "I'm sick of you breathing on my neck," pushed me face first into the icy Tremor stream. Rainbo Martin, who claimed to have "telekinetic connection" to boys, though she was fat, stood casually watching as Caro, trying to ignore it, watched her feet.

"Thanks a lot," I shouted, wringing out my coat sleeve.

"Excuse *us*," snipped Rainbo. "It's a joke—come on, man, lighten up." Caro, for her part, shrugged, and I turned and walked off in shivers through the back field of Tremor. Steven Bono, appearing eerily out of nowhere, ran after me.

Steve put a coat around my shoulders, a leopard-spotted kind of pea coat that looked as if it had survived since sixth grade. Clutching my arm a little too tightly, he said something like, "So, if a guy asked you out and if you wanted to go out with some guy that you sort of knew, if you wanted to, if I was gonna be that guy. I mean if I was gonna ask you, would you go out?"

I considered Jason, who had earlier been seen sticking Rainbo's pudgy hand down his pants. I pictured Caro, who, sensing that Jason wasn't paying attention to me, had screamed, "Rainbo likes you, Jasie," her constantly shifting allegiance like some kind of tic. I had to face facts: Jason, like every other boy I knew, abused girls. Caro, like other girls, tried to stay on the good side of boys by not objecting. The combination this time had landed me in the stream—who knew where it might get me next? Steve I could use as my bodyguard! A showpiece to parade in front of Jason! Steve was cute, I reminded myself. He had pot. "Okay, Steve," I said and, kissing him once, ran home to convince my diary that Jason was history, my parents that I had slipped by the stream while singing Beatle songs with Caro.

•   •   •

Official boyfriends—those, unlike Jason, able to predict how they would feel week to week—were cherished among all girls, celebrated as zealously, with as much peculiar ceremony, as marijuana. Just as I had created a secret stash of rolling papers (though I lacked the skill and substance for rolling joints), so I began to collect amulets that represented Steve: mementos that proved I was a girl now linked to power, to Mickey Bono, a girl who could, if nothing else, feel free to "bogart"—breaking Zappa Rule Two by keeping the righteous joint clenched between teeth and not sharing.

Within the week I told my mother that I'd be getting Steve's high school ring, as soon as he got it, plus his silver ID bracelet, plus Grateful Dead records that had belonged to Mickey. My mother closed our new dishwasher and said, "Let's not get ahead of ourselves, okay? Just when things are going so well in school and with Daddy. And who are the Grateful Dead? Who's Mickey?" Running out of the house, shouting, "Ma, you're hopeless," I carried with me a stuffed dachshund Steve had brought home once from Gettysburg, Pennsylvania. I showed it to Caro, pointing out how Steve had circled the word "Wuv" in "I Wuv Gettysburg." Caro at such moments put up a hand to say, "Okay already, Christ," followed by, "We gotta meet Rainbo. Are you coming?"

I was not. I was, within two weeks, spending every afternoon with Steve—in the Hardee's parking lot; at the pit off Sunrise—which to me seemed a logical progression in life: from Val to Caro, from Caro to the more mature, secure bond with Steve, even if this bond was kind of boring. After his initial declaration, Steve had not had much to say. Most days we would get high and then we'd sit there. I'd read, fantasize about Jason, or do Steve's homework. Steve occasionally would smirk or teach me pot tricks, such as "shotguns"—lowering his mouth over the bowl of a pipe and exhaling, he'd blow a spray of smoke back through the mouthpiece and

into my face. Then, pretending to faint from the effects, I'd
let Steve squeeze my breasts. Sometimes he'd get carried away
and pinch a nipple. Sometimes he'd pinch it too hard or say,
"I've got something big for you, babe," and I'd bolt up. "Lie
there," Steve would command, his voice sounding deep and
unfamiliar, and I'd obey, telling myself that I loved Steve,
that it was good at least to have a boyfriend, that it was at
least easier than getting jumped, or seeing my friends, who
were jealous. I'd take a hit.

If official boyfriends were worshiped, it was due largely to
how difficult things could be with other girls. It seemed suddenly that one required the analytic tools of a Kremlinologist
to decipher everyday life: who was seen standing next to
whom, in what order; who called whom, in what order; what
rumors, told in such a way, suggested possible plans of action;
which rumors, told another way, were merely fronts, deflect-
ing certain girls from guessing true intent. There were exter-
nal factors in determining status, such as which girls had
access to pot, and thus to secret funds or certain men. There
were the overriding concerns of history: Who irrationally
hated or was mad at or jealous of whom? Which girls could
the angry one count on to rally, usually two or three against
one, to her defense? Marijuana, by slowing things down,
made this process more confused—it took longer to assess the
variables, then to form an opinion. It was harder, while whispering your conclusions, to remember exactly what they
were.

Life as a whole grew complex. One afternoon in early November Steve came by to meet my family. He stood in the
kitchen wearing construction boots, dirty jeans, a linty black
sweater and, beneath that, a black Grateful Dead T-shirt. A
tattoo on his bicep—a skull and ring of red roses—was mo-

mentarily revealed as the sweater came up over his head. It
was as if his penis had popped out, then back in. I was
shocked. My sisters giggled. My father mumbled "Good day"
and walked out as my mother served tea. Steve burped and
asked for a beer.

"Gwyn," I said, pushing back my chair, "why don't you
take our picture—outside?"

We arranged ourselves as fast as we could on the lawn.
Steve stood with hands in his pockets and frowned. I clutched
his arm by the elbow, pleased to see Rainbo and Caro, passing
by on their bikes, stop to watch. Gwyn said, "Come on, you
guys—smile face." Rainbo, in a loud voice, said, "What?
Now she thinks she's Miss Purity 'cuz she has a boyfriend or
like 'cuz she's in college prep? Like no one remembers the slut
stuff you told me, right?" Caro made shushing noises. Inside
my mother made the same noises at my father, who was
shouting about "mafioso scum." I vowed not to listen to any
of them and arranged Steve's hand on my shoulder so that it
would be seen later on in the frame.

Sitting on a Zappa log several days later, I heard leaves
crunching and turned to see Steve's friend Jim, both arms
around a new girl who happened to be Val. I stared up at her
and tried to swallow. Val, who had grown breasts and dyed
her hair a yellow-blond, stared down at me.

"We meet again, Dr. Livingstone," she said with the Ger-
man accent she had claimed before was French.

Jim Scabb laughed. "So, Bono," he said, "how do you like
it that the girls here are old pals?" He laughed again and Val
laughed, causing Steve to laugh and a chill to work its way up
my spine.

Ungluing my lips to make a sound, I noticed Caro and
Rainbo coming around to stand at Val's side. Behind them
was Cyndi Fein, a wealthy Shores girl who, it was rumored,
dealt the pot she grew inside her parents' greenhouse. Because

Cyndi was Jewish I had tried once, in fifth grade, to be her friend. "Isn't it weird that everyone gets to leave early except us?" I'd said, shaking my head. Cyndi, busily combing bangs into her eyes, had said, "I don't talk to Jewish girls like you. I'm here just 'cuz I missed the catechism bus."

Cyndi's discussing me with any one of these girls would prove unnerving. All four together was frightening. Standing suddenly, I said, "I have a French test."

Steve scowled and said, "You do not. Sit down and talk to your friends like a normal fuckin' person."

I had never heard Steve speak that way before. It was the way Boat or a boy with a tattoo might speak. Steve, I remembered, *had* a tattoo. "Well," I said, nervously tripping over a rock, *"bon midi."*

Steve called, "Get back here." Rainbo glanced at Val and laughed. Cyndi Fein, passing a pink candy-striped joint to Caro, looked out at me from behind blow-dried bangs, her long, slightly crooked nose snagging her upper lip into a sneer.

In January 1973 all talk in Zappa, all gossip, shifted away from pot. In the woods, in the hallways, in the occasional phone conversation, there was talk only of acid, LSD.

What I knew about LSD, at fourteen, was limited to Health class movies in which kids turned into werewolves, then, denouncing drugs, turned back. Vaguely, from other kids, I had sensed that it was something you grew into toward age sixteen—like a junior license or a size 34 bra. But one day a ninth-grade girl I knew ran into Science shouting, "It's like Colorforms—like red and blue and shiny squiggles, patent leather, and then, after you laugh, like this clearness, like, telling you what you should do with your fucking life." This was information I badly needed. And it sounded like fun. When Steve called one January afternoon to say, "I got acid—all your friends and Cyndi are doin' it at the Unqua field, so don't make a fool outta me," I said, "Okay."

I got my hit of "windowpane"—a fancy brand, apparently —eighth period on a Friday and took it home to examine. In the envelope I found a tiny cellophane sliver. Steve had cautioned me to take only one-third of the hit, but I guessed he had been wrong. You needed a microscope to see this thing. I swallowed it whole and went downstairs to Friday night dinner.

I was telling my father about the earthworm I had cut open in Biology when my legs began to pulsate, a warm fluid like liquid sugar throbbing in the veins. The sugar quickly rose through my legs, paused in my chest as a second pulse, then ran to my head, where I felt it explode and drip slowly down, like cake batter oozing out of the pan. I was by then explaining how you had to pin back the worm's skin, and my father was discussing the advantages of taking the worm ventrally. I tried to detect whether or not he had noticed the black Magic Marker outline around my body, like the ones painted on TV sidewalks after killings. But the phone rang and he walked out, then back to say "This'll be a while," the sound of his voice trailing behind him in eighth notes you could actually see in the air. I noticed my thigh.

My jeans were covered with dusty brown patterns—I realized that they had not been washed in weeks. Perhaps it explained why Cyndi Fein did not like me: I was a secret slob, like Holden Caulfield's prep school roommate! But there was some kind of vibration near my ear. Slowly I recognized my mother's voice. She was saying "Bread?" and passing a slice across the table, successive shadows behind it like a runner over hurdles in slow motion. I took my piece of challah and brought it close to study—the amazing, unsung way small white threads had come together to create the full slice—and felt like crying for all the things in nature I had ignored. I was pressing the bread through my fingers, turning my fist to see it from all angles, when I stopped to tell my mother and sisters what, exactly, I was doing. But a blue spot appeared on the oven. There was one to the left of Sashi's head and another poised like Glinda's bubble above the sink. I said, "Would you please excuse me?"

In the bathroom mirror my face seemed to be coated with a thin layer of mud, which was revealed, upon closer inspection, to be my pancake, which led to a realization. I said: "You can always see the skin, whether the girl is pretty or a dog." At this, Gwyn opened the door and said, "What's going on with you? Dinner's almost over." I looked at her and laughed so hard I hiccuped. I touched her shoulder. I told her how very much I loved her and that she was a beautiful girl who had suffered unfairly for having been fat when she was ten.

Gwyn looked at me. She said, "What the *fuck* did you take?"

But it was time for me to leave for Unqua. I touched her shoulder, said, "Be well, Gwyn," and was off, hanging on to the doorknob, telling my mother—who squinted and said, "What's gotten into you?"—to relax, to be happy and to please, please say goodbye to Daddy.

Snow seemed to cover the Unqua field, although it had not snowed. There were Christmas bulbs on the trees, and all around me the swooshing, flapping sounds of two buses as they pass in a tunnel. I watched a gang of unusually hairy boys point at a Shores kid named Darren Shapiro, an artistic boy I had known since third grade. Darren lay on the ground shrieking, "So, kill me. Go ahead. No. Ma. Help!" I wanted to scream, "Darren, run," but Rainbo appeared with Val and we ran off to touch the green and pink flames burning like Roman candles at the edge of the field. We ran for what seemed like hours, never came close, then forgot anyway where we were supposed to be going. We rolled for a while in the old sand pit.

Rainbo sifted sand through her fingers and whispered, "The molecules of time." She smiled at Val, then rubbed my thigh. "See, it's fun," she said. "It's your first time, now don't freak on us."

I opened my mouth. What came out was my voice as it sounded on tape. "It's your first time too," this voice said.

Rainbo leaned over. She smelled like butter. "No, we do it at Cyndi's," she cooed, pinching my cheek too hard, "but no bad karma, promise?"

"Carmen who?" I asked.

"Forget it," she moaned, pulling on my arm as if rowing, "even though you have your fucking boyfriend, you're so out of it. Cyndi hates you."

Val stared at me, chewing her lower lip. I pulled on her sleeve. I said, "What's going on? It's me, Val, remember? What's going on? Please say something."

Val touched my arm and said, "It's raining." Rainbo held the other arm and said, "Cool out."

I got up, kicked sand at Rainbo and ran.

When I stopped I was on the other side of the playground. I realized that it *was* raining and that people were calling to me from the alcove by my third-grade classroom. Hoping to see Jason, I approached and saw, standing with his lips wrapped around the mouth of a beer bottle, my boyfriend, Steven Bono. There were green smears like paint beneath his eyes; he was surrounded by some girls from his neighborhood, the ones inevitably named Debbie or Karen, who studied shorthand instead of languages.

Hours seemed to pass. Finally Steve looked down at me. "Where the fuck," he said slowly, "have you been?" I was amazed: His lips hadn't moved. I tried to say, without moving mine, "Over there," and pointed out into the storm.

Steve walked to where I had pointed. He raised his bottle and threw it at the school. "I bought you this fucking acid," he shouted. "For weeks—you take my pot. You take my acid. And you don't give me what I want." The secretarial-program girls stared with open mouths as Steve, unzippering his fly, dragged me out into the rain. Coming to a stop, he shouted, "Suck it." I looked at it briefly, then ran instead, holding my stomach, which suddenly ached, hoping I'd pass one of the Roman candles. I pictured throwing it onto the field, and everyone—except poor Darren, whom I would save—shouting "Fuckin' A!" as they exploded in one pink and fizzy flame. But the only light was the dim haze of street lamps on wet pavement. The rain continued. I held my stomach and ran home.

The following Wednesday, the ninth grade was scheduled to view *Animal Farm,* the animated version, at 9:00 A.M. in the auditorium. At 8:00 A.M. in Zappa, Boat Brody, who'd been hit by a car and slightly brain damaged, announced that he had "brown dot"—a type of "blotter" acid, in which the drug is concentrated in a liquid dot on a tiny slip of paper. Standing on a log, throwing LSD squares into the air, he shouted: "Fuckin' go on! The fuckin' animals talk! *They fuckin' talk!*"

Word traveled fast, and by first period a wobbly line stretched from woods to cafeteria door. I pushed my way through it in search of Steve. I had decided that I would leave him for a boy in college prep: Enough, as my father had shouted when I'd come home the acid night "freaking drunk again," was enough. Weaving between girls, their tongues held out snakelike for a hit, a few guys hanging moons, I ran into Caro.

She had her own hit, a fifteenth-birthday gift from a friend of her brother's. Caro said she'd planned to split it with Rainbo but, since she hadn't seen me in a while, said she'd share it with me. The idea of tripping in school was about as appealing as tripping at my grandmother's. But I would need to have Caro back as a friend when I left Steve. Promising myself I'd do extra homework that night, I took the half-hit and ran inside behind her.

Sometime later we found the auditorium. It seemed to be empty. After half an hour had passed, we determined that the film had been canceled. A group of girls who had not yet figured this out stood licking their lips. There was a kid fingering the trophy case and one crouched by the double glass doors, amazed by the way his shoelaces could be tied, then untied. Ahead in the main hall I heard poor Darren Shapiro.

"They said there would be animals," he sobbed. A crowd gathered by the staircase where he crouched. A teacher rolled up his sleeves, shouting, "I'll need help," and a boy with short hair and bell-bottoms hemmed above the ankle emerged from the crowd. "Sir," he called out, "I'll be glad to alert the authorities." I recognized fake-Cousin Donnie, stared at him, my heart expanding like a wet sponge beneath the skin, and then ran.

I got as far as the stream before I collapsed. Sitting on the bank, rubbing my arms, I tried, as Rainbo would say, to be in tune with my environment. I compared the way the water flowed toward Zappa with the way kids crammed onto the stairs between periods, then disappeared. But as I was considering this cosmic unity, and whether or not it could be true that Jason fucked Cyndi on her waterbed, Steve walked up, placed a sneaker on my thigh and pushed.

He instantly began screaming—about what a disappointment I was, about how nobody ever knew what the fuck went on in my skull. His face was changing color, like a cartoon volcano in a Science class film. Watching it, I longed for a raft so that I could float quickly through Zappa, under Merrick Road, out toward the sinking barge and then the bay. Steve perhaps sensed this. Shoving my shoulder, he said, "You are not fucking even listening to me. No one fucking listens to me, goddammit." He sat down and sighed.

I was about to say, "It's over. Tell it to someone else," when Steve began to speak, enunciating as carefully as an angry cop. "You better watch out," he said, "and you better tell your old man to watch out. I could come to your house some night, I could smash the glass in your cute picture window. Your family — your snotty little Nassau Shores family — is gonna be in big trouble if you don't watch it. Now you listen."

I put my fingers in my ears. Steve pulled them out. "This is it," he shouted. "I'm tired of waiting around. I gotta get laid. Jim and Ken have been getting it for months — though you wouldn't know that because you have no fucking friends."

I wanted to say, "Who's Ken getting it with?" or "How do you know?" and mostly "If you touch my family, I'll have you killed." Instead, I started crying. Steve put his arm around me. He sighed again and said that things in his life weren't that good, and that someday he would tell me specifically why. For now, however, he needed my body. I had to understand. I was fourteen. He was fifteen. "I'm not gettin' any younger," he said.

I reviewed my present life. I pictured my friends, one at a time, and all the things that they had done without me — acid, sex, who knew what? I pictured fake-Cousin Donnie and then Steve. I pictured saying "Fuck off" to Steve, who'd break into my house with a gun.

Turning to face him, I said, "Do whatever you want, you asshole."

One white winter day in February of 1973, I rode my bicycle to Steven Bono's. We went into his garage, put on gas masks and inhaled hashish that Steve had stolen from a friend of his brother's. When the garage looked like the scene of a brush fire, we walked into the house, past the Jesus, which now hung alongside a fuzzy mallard duck embroidery, past Steve's mother, who waved from the kitchen, where she sat surrounded by Steve's little brothers, Craig, Charlie and Anthony. Waving back, I followed Steve up the long, narrow flight of stairs to his attic room.

It was tiny, decorated with dark wood paneling and nautical-theme curtains. There were bookshelves that held beer mugs. A Confederate flag hung from the ceiling like a parachute; a mattress lay at an angle on the floor. Steve closed the door, wedged an old lacrosse stick beneath the handle, then began to grab at the strings of my white gauze shirt. I pushed him away. "What about your mother?" I asked.

"Just be quiet," Steve whispered as he pulled the shirt over my head. I covered my breasts. He turned to fumble with his silver skull belt buckle. I watched the rug, a red-and-black shag embedded with pot seeds and bits of Oreo cookie. When I looked up, Steve's penis was stretching against his underwear and one second later it came springing out into the room, like a high-diving board after you've leapt. Quickly he pulled off my pants and rolled me down onto the floor, pinning my arms back over my head. My eyes were level with some black ants transporting Oreo crumbs across the carpet. I noticed some transparent red ants crawling on a Frito by the outlet and wondered if red ants were more attracted to salt than black ants. I closed my eyes and pictured Jason as Steve wiggled his hips between my legs and pressed, pressing harder until I thought I heard flesh rip. I pictured my father. It ripped more severely and I pictured Nanny Etta, my Jewish grandmother, and the way she tore the pimply yellow skin off a chicken. At last, minutes later, Steve flopped to one side, forming a heap next to the mattress to match the pile of clothes near the chair.

He said, "Far out, babe," lifted one arm and slapped the rug. I said, "I have to set the table," and raced around gathering my clothes, trying to get my head through the peasant top as I pulled on my jeans. Wiping my hands on my pants, I stepped over Steve into the hallway, sunshine through a storm window slapping my cheek.

At home my mother looked at the clock, pursed her lips and handed me a stack of five plates. When I'd gotten them suitably arranged, I walked into the bathroom and washed my hands for half an hour. I came out to talk to Steve on the phone.

"How's the little sex goddess?" he asked.

"Steve," I hissed, "are you completely crazy? Don't you ever say that to me on the phone. And I'm bleeding."

He said, "You belong to me now, babe," and I shivered and focused on a dresser-top photo of me at the annual Brownie father-daughter spaghetti lunch. Steve made slurping noises at the other end of the phone, my mother called me down for dinner, and I sat there, recalling how, despite an army of bobby pins, I had never been able to keep the Brownie beanie on my head.

By the start of my sophomore year I had been having sex —in Steve's mother's car; behind the nearly completed mall on the pit—a full seven months. I had not exactly come to love Steve. But loving a regular pot supply and his protection, afraid mostly of what he'd do if I said no, I'd cut a deal: I would let him do it if he would get me very high beforehand, giving me extra pot to share with Gwyn and Coco, our dog, whom we'd walk for two hours each night, when he was through. Also, he had to take me to the movies. Also, we had to follow a "rhythm" calendar I kept in the margins of my diary, modeled on the one I'd read about in *Glamour* magazine.

My friends, I assumed, had made similar arrangements.

We were all turning fifteen that fall of 1973. Shags and ponytails had given way to a neater style: hair curled under at the shoulder, then curled up, banana-shaped, at the bang. We wore shiny wet strawberry lip gloss, Huk-A-Poo tops—fakesilk blouses with pointy collars and cuffs—and baggy carpenter's pants over striped socks and suede Earth Shoes. We were dressing up, trying to look older for boys.

Val claimed to be pre-engaged to Jim Scabb; Rainbo had "a bond" to Ken Puglia, whom she'd renamed Moonchild; people claimed that Cyndi Fein let Jason, whom I still loved, deal her pot. Even Caro had a boyfriend. It was Boat. Coordinating clothes, comparing the bulky rings and thin ankle bracelets they collected as gifts, girls behaved that fall like teens on a 1960s TV show. Forgiven temporarily, as Rainbo said, "for flauntin' Steve and bein' a snob about college prep," I was allowed to play along—grabbing coffee at the Nautilus Diner on Merrick, piercing ears, then shrieking, lamenting the way boys tended to swallow without chewing. But no matter how many slumber parties I snorted speed for, I still did not know if my friends had sex, just as I still did not know when they'd first dropped LSD. It seemed you couldn't ask.

In the eighth and ninth grades, sex had hung suspended over conversation like a canvas tent about to giddily collapse.

By the tenth grade, however, all talk, all innuendo, had gone underground. The moral code governing such matters was far too hard to read: A girl who had actual sex might be admired *or* reviled, depending on how she ranked during a given week in terms of men; pot supply; appeasement of opposing girl forces; the number of secrets known and bartered. As sex became a real possibility, girls—not wishing to contend both with intercourse *and* this hostile rating system—ceased to discuss it at all.

It was also true, of course, that no one said that much about anything. We had, by late 1973, been stoned nearly every day for a year. Life—the swath cut from home to school to woods—had taken on a listless quality that in a Health class film might have been depicted by a long-haired boy with his head down on a desk. It was entirely possible to sit for hours with another couple, to walk home with Gwyn, carrying the dog, and exchange not one word.

It was also entirely possible, I wrote in my diary, that my friends just did not wish to discuss sex, or anything important, with *me*. It seemed possible that Val and Caro had all kinds of sex, took notes and compared; Cyndi might have had a negligee or a stash of acid she shared with Rainbo, who seemed now to flirt with Jason! The most popular phrase around school that term was "paranoid delusion." The newly available drug was THC—the active ingredient in marijuana packaged in a handy pill form. THC, from what I gathered, made you feel as if a thin, quivering membrane hung poised between you and the world. When that passed, it gave you a headache, then made you nervous. Two cheerleaders I knew had stolen 700 hits from a dealer and sold them all winter outside a 7-Eleven by the half-sunken barge. On March 15, because I'd helped with her French homework, one of them gave me a hit. Swallowing it, moving immediately to the "nervous" phase, I sat at the center of my mother's rock garden, telling Sashi, who asked, "Why are you sitting in the leaves?", that I was "trying to shed paranoia and fear."

But there was good reason, that spring of 1974, to feel nervous. Steve, for one, seemed out of control. He had failed out of Spanish class and dropped out of Shop. Stepping off a curb one day, he'd broken his ankle and, with the cast still on, drove his brother's car into a bush. At home any night my father was likely to scream, storm out of rooms or pull the plug from the TV. The steel business he ran with Uncle Benny was slow, said my mother. He was nearly fifty, she'd tell us, he was tired and tense, as we could see: The lower buttons of his shirt strained against a newly sprung belly; his hairline had receded to expose veins in his head resembling tiny tree roots.

In May he hung up the phone on Steve, who had been caught "streaking" naked through a Typing class. In July he stood at dinner to announce that I, "his eldest, beloved child," was "standing around idly with scum," while no one "freaking paid attention." He walked out of the house, Sashi cried, and we spoke again only in August, on the day Richard Nixon resigned. I spoke that same historic week to Steve, who had been busted and sent to live with Mickey for three months at his college. Back in school that fall, people smoked hash openly in the hallways. Someone tried to sell me a mood ring without the stone. One of the Beatles, John, had his picture in *Newsday;* he had been thrown out of an L.A. nightclub while wearing a sanitary napkin glued to his forehead.

I was depressed. I was lonely. The communal fun of couples had faded. Other girls had earned junior licenses to drive and cruised town in cars they'd borrowed or, like Cyndi, received as gifts. My mother refused to consider this. My father, who had hollered one night, "You dig your own grave," was again not speaking to me at all. On my sixteenth birthday, I went to the guidance office and copied the names and addresses of 100 colleges out of a catalogue. I asked my mother for stamps and sent away for brochures and applications, then went to see Val, whose mother, like mine, had said "absolutely no" to the license.

We walked to school the next day, commiserating. We walked to the Nautilus Diner every morning after that and, on the first warm night of spring 1975, to see *American Graffiti,* which we had missed two years before due to its rating. On the way back through the Mays parking lot, walking down the secret path that led to the park, I asked, "Do you ever wish you could live in another time?"

I expected Val to say, "What the fuck are you talking about?" but she surprised me by nodding. "Why would anybody want to be living now?" she said, shrugging. "It's so totally boring." She offered me gum.

"I'm so thrilled I'll be leaving for college," I said. "I can't wait."

Val spit out her gum, explaining that it tasted like mouthwash. She said, "I'll probably live at home and be a secretary."

I shook my head and spit out my gum alongside hers. "Who would have thought it'd turn out this way?" I said.

"Really," said Val, and we sat on a bench by the community pools smoking a joint, talking about the happier days of sixth grade, before we had entered this sad phase of life.

My senior year at Tremor High, Steve left to study catering at a junior college near Oswego, New York. I became re-attached to Val. We spent mornings in the Nautilus Diner drinking coffee the color of caramel, listening ten times to the David Bowie song "Changes" as we stared romantically out at the barge. Afternoons we spent in her den, where Val drew "disco" designs for prom dresses and I filled out the college applications my mother reviewed with me each night. Caro came by on some days and we drove—to the mall; past the Amityville house where Ron DeFeo, a former Tremor drug dealer, had shot and killed his family; then back to Val's to get out and inspect our oldest records. We were, like girls everywhere, sentimental, given to strange, abrupt confessions.

"You know," Caro said, blowing smoke in my face one day at lunch, "I never told you, but you have really great eyes."

I'd done well on my SATs. I had my license. Relax, I'd tell myself, trying to smile at my father, You are leaving for college.

Still, there were things in life that made me nervous.

One of the secretarial-program girls we knew had gotten pregnant the winter before and had either ignored it or secretly wanted to have a baby or possibly, I thought, hadn't noticed. That November she appeared in school, only one month to go. Lined up at bathroom mirrors, in Gym, on Zappa logs, girls assessed her situation—rating her in terms of circumstance, attitude about self ("you know, is she like stuck up?"), pot supply, creative maternity clothes. She was a nice girl, it was determined, a little dumb; they'd give her a shower in Cyndi's greenhouse.

Personally I was shocked. It had never occurred to me that any girl I knew could just get pregnant. It was something that seemed to apply to older girls, to wives, even if it did seem more likely that a secretarial girl end up this way than a girl bound for college. I mentioned the pregnant girl one day to my mother just to see if she agreed. She looked at me as if I'd asked if we could please be Catholic. "That is absolutely outrageous," she said. "A girl of seventeen has no business fooling around with such serious things, Betsy. Now, you're leaving soon for college. You just steer clear of this stuff and get your work done."

Taking my mother's cue, I told Rainbo, who'd planned the shower, that I thought the girl was a moron. "I have no time for stupid things like this," I said, "I'm leaving for college." Slapping her contributions envelope against one thigh, Rainbo hissed, "I hope you never get in trouble, you fucking snob. 'Cuz there ain't gonna be no one there to dig you out."

Rainbo, I figured, was not leaving home and thus felt jealous. The shower went ahead without me the following week. The girl put her baby up for adoption the week after, and I moved on to other worries, mainly finding part-time work.

The year before, I'd had a job at a fruit stand but had been fired for lying to the boss about my age. I'd since then become afraid to ask for work, imagining as I approached stores that the girls behind counters, the ones who had not been fired, would start laughing—at my clothes, perhaps, or because I lacked experience. When I'd talk myself into asking, I'd stand there stammering until someone said, "Okay, we'll call you." Back at home I'd sit in the playroom, too embarrassed to call Val, who worked as a waitress, or Caro, who'd been hired at Carlucci's Hardware. Frustrated, I'd tell Gwyn, who played piano for my mother's ballet classes, how soon I would be leaving.

One spring day I broke the long silence with my father to talk to him about college. After rehearsing with my mother, I announced the names of the five private schools I'd been accepted at, placing a brochure on the table after each name. My father, his mouth twisted tight as a corkscrew, sat staring straight ahead.

To get things rolling I said, "Look, I'll be leaving Steve, okay? Just not until after the prom."

My father cleared his throat. "It's a miracle that you've made it this far," he said, "more of one that you have any grade point average at all."

"Look," I said, unfolding brochures from the two schools I favored. "Either one will be fine."

My father shrugged. "I'm sorry," he said. "I'm afraid your mother has been a bit overly optimistic. We simply cannot afford these schools. You should have come to me while you were applying. That way, you'd have kept your sights on something more within our range."

While I was applying, I nearly shouted, *you were telling me to dig my own grave.* I managed to smile. I tried another, smaller school in Boston.

"Nope," he said, handing it back.

"What?" I whined. "What do you want me to do?"

"A state school," he said. "Apply for scholarships. Get a job to help out with expenses once you're there."

I ran up to my room in tears, convinced that my only true form of communication had been with a notebook idiotically named Dear Best Friend. A while later my mother came in with the brochures I'd received from the state universities, and we looked at them together. Calverton, an arts and sciences college somewhere far off by Rochester, seemed nicest: small, with sculptures and skywalks and the kinds of lawns and brick buildings I had dreamed of. I applied, was accepted, though it was late, and hung pictures of the Humanities building where I'd once had a picture of Steve.

"Now all you have to do," my mother said, brushing the back of my hair, "is to survive the end of senior year."

For the senior prom most everyone thought we should do MDA; on senior day, people said, "STP's the way to go." No one in the end was that particular. Dealers walked around in front of the school with shoe boxes full of whatever was available. Girls opened their purses and shoveled the stuff inside; guys made Black Power fists, said, "All right, bro," and got back inside jacked-up Camaros. On May 1 banners announcing "Smokin' '76" and "Hawaiian or Bust" appeared tangled in the branches high above Zappa. By June there was sand in the halls and kids you barely knew coming over to make the *mwah* kissing sound as they dropped limp arms onto your shoulders.

At home my mother worked on my prom dress—a sparkling salmon-colored halter gown we'd found pictured in Butterick patterns. I painted pale silver starfish onto Val's nails. Gwyn tried unsuccessfully to curl Caro's hair, and at last it was time for "Sunset of Memories," the big event for the 730-member bicentennial class. Steve, wearing a lavender tux with a red shirt, sat in a rented Cadillac outside my house that night and burst into tears.

"What?" I asked, "Did your dog die?"

Steve took a shaky breath. He said, "My old man split—a while ago. I guess you noticed by now. My parents are getting separated. My father's gonna live with some bitch. My mother's drinking. She fell and broke her ankle, like I broke my ankle the first day he stormed out. Mickey has to move back for a while. I'm not even gonna have my own room. I'll have to share with Anthony. He fucking wets the bed." Steve let his head drop onto the steering wheel.

"Oh, my God," I said, "Steve, when did all this happen? When you broke your ankle? When was that? I can't even remember."

Steve said, "Two years ago."

I sat there, shocked. Finally I said, "You are with me now, Steve. And this will be your night. Steve, I am your girlfriend. We will have the best time in history."

Steve sniffled and pulled two beers out of a cooler in the

backseat. Opening mine as we drove, I tried to remember the sex calendar I had drawn in my diary for June. I was pretty sure it was an "X" day—a dangerous "no sex" day, although I couldn't quite remember. But what could happen? It was the fuckin' senior prom! Steve needed me. I was going to leave him for someone more my type, maybe Jason, if he'd take me. It was the least that I could do.

The next week, we received our yearbooks. Over her picture, Caro asked that I remember *the daze we hung around by the pools, the PIT, the liquor store, the stream, the park, the diner. When Hils ate Ben-Gay and you carved your arm . . . we have been friends 5 years, 1 month, 24 days and we will always be friends, now and forever, like the Mersey Marvels, our heroes, forever, the Beatles.* I felt like crying. Val recalled *Kiddles and Trolls, playin' spin the pencil, the time Nanny Florita taught us the dance "This is the world of Mod,"* then went on for pages to cite the meaningful objects and people we had known: *the milk pitcher that talked at Coco's, our pet the shopping cart, Italian ices at the old White's, the "fruits of the world" bulletin board, the hangers we put yarn on, the dead bird in the drive-in, loving Paul. Nair.* I was crying. Rainbo Martin wrote *I sure there a million memories, but I can't think of them right now.*

That night I went to play miniature golf with Steve, Caro and Boat, who had a new tattoo featuring Jerry Garcia and the Creature from the Black Lagoon on a motorcycle. We brought Gwyn and Steve's little brother Craig, along with a quarter-ounce of hash, and some champagne sent by Mickey, who now worked at a bank in New Jersey. After spending half an hour on the same windmill, we went to the famous Root-beer Dog on Jericho Turnpike to get shakes. I announced my plans for the future and everyone at the table, even Boat and Steve, cheered.

The next night I went to visit Val, whose longtime love, Jim, had gone into the navy to study boiler repair. We reviewed our lives in 45s: "Simon Says" by the 1910 Fruitgum Company, "Red Rubber Ball" by the Cyrkle, "Incense and Peppermints" by the Strawberry Alarm Clock; someone impersonating Paul McCartney singing "Yesterday" like The Chipmunks; someone impersonating Bobby Kennedy singing "Wild Thing." I went home at 2:00 A.M. to write about how happy I was: I'd gone to the prom and looked great! I'd gone to the beach since and looked better! My father had made me a starry blue painting of Mont-St.-Michel, a place he'd seen during the war. He'd written on the back *for a dream yet to come true,* which I took as a sign of the future. I'd just come home from Val's, where I'd gotten in touch with the past.

I'd also, probably the night of the prom, gotten pregnant.

F O U R

The first thing I noticed graduation morning was Val's sundress: It was striped just like mine, with the same plunging neck, little bow and open back. The difference was that hers fit. Mine I'd had to force at the zipper, so that my breasts were pushed together like two hand-balls. Flab like my grandmother's had gathered, dimpled, by the armpit. Watching Val tug on a loose shoulder strap made me dizzy, and I sat down where I was on a step.

A small crowd quickly gathered at my feet. My mother, holding out her hand, said, "Time for pictures." Val said, "Don't just sit there." Sashi said, "Come on." They were staring at me, Gwyn pointed to the door, and so, my stomach sucked in, I walked out onto the lawn to pose for photos: white gowns on; gowns off; next to mothers; fathers; sisters; grandparents; Val and me and Coco. I said to myself, Relax. So you gained a little weight. Everything else is beautiful. Champagne was passed around in plastic cups. Polaroids were compared. Our mothers actually hugged, and at last Val and I walked off for the final time toward school.

Three hours later, in ninety-degree heat, the class of '76 stood to toss hats into the air. I reached for mine and discovered that I'd lost it. I had also lost Val. I'd lost my parents. Caro, across the gym, hugged Cyndi Fein. Absently I hugged the girl next to me and wandered out past Zappa, almost in tears, which was inevitable, I assumed, considering the emotional intensity of this day.

Relatives and neighbors clapped as I walked back into the yard. I smiled. I said, "Oh you know, I feel pretty much the same," but I felt sick. Waves of dizziness popped like tiny piano hammers against my forehead; even my waist seemed to be sweating. Sitting down, I wondered if I'd caught a contact high from all the pot smoked back in the gym: The air looked watery, gasoline-streaked with the heat of the barbecue; people seemed to move through it in slow motion. I noticed my mother's parents, Florita and Gus, coming toward me, but like two mimes pumping their arms to convey movement. At last, minutes later, they stood at my side. My grandmother, smiling, held out a package. Smiling back, I grabbed it and, though my hands shook, unwrapped a round silver tray that had my initials engraved at the center.

"We gave you silver from Tiffany's, Betsy, when you turned ten," recalled Nanny Florita, "and it seemed time to repeat the gesture now that you're, well, how old are you these days?"

"Seventeen," I said, tears wedged like a knee sock in my throat. "I'm seventeen."

When I looked up again they had gone; Nanny Etta, my father's mother, now stood in their place. I thought of the ghosts changing shifts in *A Christmas Carol*. Etta winked and pulled a package from her purse. "Grown-up lady hankies," she told me.

I placed the hankies on the tray. I said, "They're beautiful, Nanny," and ran with them inside to the bathroom, where I was sure I'd either faint or throw up. But on the way I bumped into my father. He was carrying three green wine bottles, which he placed with emphasis one at a time onto the couch. Taking hold of my shoulders, he said, "I have saved this champagne thirty years, since the war, for such an occasion."

I accepted one bottle, kissed him and backed away sort of bowing, like a Japanese person who has not yet learned the American way to end a conversation. I had backed out again, holding bottle, hankies and tray, into the yard. I smiled at the company. I worked at peeling the label—which said 1966—and said to myself, You feel goddamned fine. But looking up, I noticed Steve, holding one of the champagne bottles to his lips. My stomach lurched. Steve grabbed my arm. "We got a party to go to," he said in a voice so loud my mother a few feet off clearly heard it. Removing the bottle from Steve's hands, she said, "Only for a little while, sweetheart, there are people here who want to see you," a hint I hoped Steve would take. But Steve frowned, said, "We gotta go," and pulled me away to his car.

In a backyard far across the tracks, I sat at a picnic table watching a mother wearing a corsage on her wrist carry out a cake. In shiny blue script it said, *Congratulations, Vincent. We are very proud of you.* A kid sitting across from me looked quizzically at the cake, as if it were the first one he'd ever seen. Then, snorting, he sent his fist down through the center. Unexpectedly, I started to cry. Caro and Cyndi looked at me and then at Steve, who said, "Ya gotta excuse her, she's over-emotional," and pulled me out to the sidewalk.

"It's your fuckin' graduation," he shouted, as a girl on the lawn began to puke. "Why don't you try to get into it?"

"Because I want to go home," I said, "this dress is killing me. I miss my mother."

Steve let go of the arm he had been clutching. "You're a fucking faggot," he pronounced.

"I'm sorry," I said and, ignoring his shouts, began to run. At home one hour later, I ripped the dress getting it off, kicked the material into a corner and exhaled.

My father had gone to drive Nanny Etta home to Brooklyn. My grandfather had fallen asleep in a chair. My mother, coming up from the playroom, looked around, shrugged and poured the last of the World War II champagne. Drinking it from Dixie cups, my sisters and I scraped plates, pretending to sing "La Vie en Rose" in French. We put a bow on the dog and competed at doing the best arabesque while holding the refrigerator handle. Nanny Florita judged. Sashi won three times, and Gwyn poured one last tiny cup of champagne over her head.

By the time I helped my mother out with the trash at 10:00 P.M. I felt like a happier, more compassionate, more useful person, the person I was supposed to have been all along. I would leave Steve. I would just leave.

One of the paper plates I stuffed inside a bag had writing on it—Nanny Etta's. I had barely spoken to her, hoping to avoid the lecture on why I shouldn't go so far from home, what Gwyn called "the updated 'What-Will-Happen-If-You-Do-Anything' speech." Apparently Etta had noticed. In her best penmanship she'd recorded on her plate *Today, 6/28/76, I attended Betsy's graduation. It was lonely.* I dropped the bag, stepped on a pink plastic fork and ran upstairs to my room.

I sat up most of the night shivering—from all the excitement, I thought, or as a result of the sadness that accompanied change. In the morning my father came in with a map of New York State to show me where, in August, I'd be going. We studied possible routes. It was thrilling to picture. But there was the whole summer to get through first.

My routine July days consisted of this: At 8:00 A.M. I'd condition my hair, timing the rinse on the silver watch I'd received for graduation. At 8:20, after tying a red Indian-print skirt over a black leotard and preparing two precise banana curls, I'd walk downstairs, set to find a summer job.

My mother had agreed to give me the station wagon every day for as long as it took. She'd rehearse with me what I would say and then walk me out to the car, calling *"Merde"*— the traditional dancer's slang for "good luck." Driving off, I'd feel confident. Waiting for a light at Sunrise, however, I'd start to sweat.

Actually getting a job was hard to picture. I was still unnerved by having to ask: A boss might learn that I'd been fired and then fire me again! Or I might get stuck while counting change, just as I had doing word problems, forgetting midway through the process how it was exactly that you finished. And I felt oddly apathetic. After years of hanging around, years of the wrong and boring friends, it seemed that there was nothing left to do but to leave, to start brilliantly, energetically over as soon as possible. The only point of the present was to wait, and I was content to do this, to read novels, without the anxiety of asking for work.

But it was hard to explain this view to other people. My mother, holding my hand, would say, "I have complete faith that you'll find a job soon." My father would say, "Quit wasting time. You just get out there and do it." Nearly everyone else I knew seemed too busy to discuss what I was or wasn't doing. Steve had gotten a summer job in New Jersey sorting mail at Mickey's bank. Val had met an older man named Victor. Canceling a beach date, she'd explained that Victor, who was tall, had sat at her waitress's station two weeks straight to watch her "work like a poem with the sponge." Canceling again, she'd said, "He's twenty-five. He has a fucking boat!" I'd tried to ask Caro about this Victor. But driving past Carlucci's Hardware each night, I'd see Caro's old blue Valiant pulling out behind Boat's Charger, which drove behind Jason's Pinto, which as a rule had Rainbo, feet up, in the front.

Reminding myself that I hated them, secretly feeling abandoned, I'd drive on.

One early July day, leotard soaked, banana flip wilting, I drove on to Route 135, a long, usually empty stretch of highway connecting South Shore to North. It was the road that led to the parkways toward the city, the road I would be driving in August. Hitting the gas and cranking the AM, I drove once in each direction before driving home. I did the same thing every day thereafter, glancing at store windows on Sunrise for "Help Wanted" signs, picturing Calverton as it had looked in the brochures. In seven weeks, I'd tell myself, waving at my mother, who'd walk across the lawn to meet me, I would be in that brochure, a free girl with real friends and an interesting life.

To prove to myself that I was actually leaving, I began to shop for toiletries at the West Massapequa Pathmark. Gwyn helped me fill blue baskets with cotton balls, eyelash curlers and tampons, then to pile things against a wall in my room according to type of item or its size.

One day, driving to shop for nail polish and polish remover, I felt dizzy and hot, then rapidly cold and then hot again—exactly how I'd felt at graduation. I pulled over.

"What is it?" asked Gwyn.

Gripping the dashboard, I said, "Oh you know, I had the flu last winter. It must be some kind of carry-over or something."

Gwyn squinted her eyes. "I know what it is," she said. "It's probably that you're nervous to leave home."

"I'm not nervous, Gwyn," I said defensively. "It's time to leave. But maybe, maybe it's that my body is acting out on its own. You know, I am not nervous psychologically, but my body senses the change chemically."

"Yeah," she said. "That's what I meant. It's a big change. I'm sure you're gonna have some nerves."

I thought about how my hands lately had been so sweaty they slid off the wheel as I drove. "Yeah," I said, flipping on the radio, "you're probably right." And I wiped my palms on the edges of the pillow I sat on to drive, smiled at my sister, who was staring, and pulled out.

I was driving one day, the second week in July, when it occurred to me that I hadn't had my period. Struggling to keep the car in lane, I tried to recall whether or not I'd gotten it in June. I remembered having it, although that might have been May, which then very suddenly had become June and then July. "Look," I said out loud, "it doesn't mean a thing" —even in less exciting times my period had been erratic, showing up one month at the beginning, the next time at the end, forcing me constantly to revise the chart in my diary margins. "Look," I said, turning onto 135, "it is always here soon enough." I hit the gas, pressing the accelerator the way you might the pedal of an electric guitar. My period, I was sure, would appear "with a vengeance," two months' worth in August, to ruin my final days in this life.

The following week, I was sitting in the kitchen, drawing my mother a diagram of the dorm, when the feeling I'd had at graduation returned.

Watching the color drain from my face, she asked, "Honey, what's wrong? Are you coming down with something?"

"What are you talking about?" I said, peeling her hand from my forehead. "I'm fine. I'm totally fine. Besides, even if there was something slightly wrong, it couldn't really be anything serious because I have always been fine, you know that. Plus," I added, getting up to stretch, "it's doubly unlikely anything would happen now, you know, for me to get sick, since I'm leaving."

She was watching me. "Oh, Mom," I said, "I'm just a little nervous. I feel better already."

"Is it your period?" she asked.

"Mother, I am fine," I snapped, backing up the stairs. "Get off my case. Okay?"

Lying face down in the beanbag, vomit burning at the back of my throat, I called out that I was sorry and that I was fine. I reminded myself that I had, every year, passed my physical with Dr. Leonard—a heavy, red-cheeked man with white shoes and a buh-buh-buh Bing Crosby style of humming he'd interrupt to say "Watch the clown" as he jammed a needle into your arm. For days after we'd be limp with fear, returning to normal only after the TB-test Band-Aid had come off and it was clear that we would live. And now, as then, I would live. My period would come. I certainly could not ask Dr. Leonard where it was. I sat up in the beanbag chair. I opened my diary and closed it. I went shopping.

Still, it was July 20, and I was nervous. Although I would not tell my sisters why, I went to the bathroom four times an hour. There I had evolved a routine: Closing my eyes, I would lower myself carefully onto the toilet, as I had as a child playing "Helen Keller's House." In this updated version of the game, I kept one hand over my underwear as I sat, letting each eye flutter slowly open. That way the first traces of red would be joyously vague, as the first trace of LSD was a mere dot that turned into a spectrum. But my underwear betrayed me every time. I had always been lucky, I told myself. Watching goose pimples erupt on my thigh, I'd say, This will pass.

But it did not, July was almost over, and I was losing patience with the Helen Keller routine. I checked for blood while driving in traffic with one hand; I checked in the damp gray bathrooms of Tobay Beach and once in Sam Goody's classical cassettes section, which was all the way at the back and always empty. I set a deadline—July 25—for my period to come; when it did not, I allowed myself an extension and started talking to myself as I drove. One late July day I talked myself into driving on 135 the two or three towns up to Hempstead.

There was a place there I'd heard mentioned on the radio

called the Bill Bear clinic or the Bill Beard or Bird clinic—
the Bill Somebody clinic. I did not know exactly where the
Bill clinic was; I did not know anyone who'd actually gone or
what you were supposed to ask for once you got there, though
it would, I was pretty sure, concern abortion.

On July 30 I stopped at a gas station and called information, but there was no listing under Bear or Beard or Bird.
Exasperated, I hung up and called back a minute later. It
sounded like the same operator. I hung up. It would be
smarter, I decided, just to drive around the town. Perhaps I'd
simply see it. I tried but I did not see it, and was not sure
what I'd have done if I had. It would be harder to ask for this,
whatever I was asking for, than it would be to ask for a job. I
had no money of my own. My parents had no money—it was
all going toward college—so I could not ask them, and my
mother was disappointed as it was. "No luck with jobs?"
she'd say, "Are you sure you looked everywhere?" My father
had accused me of abandoning my flute and ballet. I pictured
Gwyn at the piano. I pictured Sashi, who was only ten, and
then Caro, and the way she would rush to tell Jason, who'd
never love me then, or Boat, who would tell Ken Puglia or
Jim Scabb, who would tell Steve, who would say, "You fucking idiot," provided my father hadn't run him over first with
the car. And what if somehow I got the money without my
parents or Steve, who made me sick? They would surely ask
for identification at the Bill place. I wasn't twenty-one; I
wasn't even eighteen.

One day, the first week of August, my car swerved off the
road. I sat, stunned, at the side of Route 135, inhaling a
Wash 'n Dri I'd pulled from the crease of the seat. Two hours
later I sat parked in an alley near my house, the smell of
ammonia faintly in the air, smudged Wash 'n Dris littering
the floor. One lay across my face. Removing it, I walked
inside the Nassau Shores candy store, where the senile owners

seemed to think I was still one of the cute neighborhood kids.
I asked for the *Village Voice,* a newspaper from the city. They
did not have it, but the man gave me in its place a free
Charms lollipop because I "looked so sad." I thanked him,
picked up *Newsday* and carried it, with the lollipop, back to
the car. Anxiously I searched for words relating to my situation.

Toward the end of the classifieds I came at last to the word
"abortion." It was in a column marked "21 and Over." In the
far bottom right corner of the page I might have seen a small
display ad for the Bill Baird Center of Hempstead, "call
today . . . confidentiality guaranteed." But I never got that
far. Exhausted, I had let my head flop back against the seat.

In honor of my leaving, fake-Aunt Ruth had asked me out
to lunch, a date I had dreaded for weeks. As the mother of the
prodigious Donnie and Lisette, Ruth had long felt duty-
bound to remind me that I was a "nonachiever"—for some
Jewish mothers of the area, a social designation equivalent
roughly with that of "public masturbator." During the past
year she had expressed her dismay by asking about schools,
then, as I answered, folding her hands to say, "Sweetie, you
really don't have the outside activities for something of that
caliber." But it was August 10, I told myself. I was leaving. I
had to say goodbye to those who had been with me in this
life.

As we drove down Merrick Road Aunt Ruth said, "You'll
have to tell me at lunch all about your little state school." But
I could not wait. I started in with amazing lies about the
campus—how in every suite there were baby grand pianos
with velvet-fringed seat covers; how there were color TVs in
the rooms and cars that came to get you for class. Ruth said,
"Why, it sounds lovely for a state school. How nice for you,"

and proceeded to describe the Yale campus, where Donnie was, as of the day before, "at university."

Aunt Ruth said she had to stop before lunch at a bakery. I nodded and followed her inside, my stomach audibly gurgling. I said to myself that being with Aunt Ruth had just upset it, and attempted to concentrate on cookies: the black/white moons we'd had as Thursday after-school treats; the powdery white tarts everyone except my father hated; the popular pink Italian cookies, finger-shaped, half-dipped in chocolate. Aunt Ruth ordered a dozen of these. I turned and threw up at her feet. Some junior high girls ran out, giggling. Aunt Ruth said, "Oh, God," grabbed her cookies and hustled me out to the car.

Sounding like Jack Webb on "Dragnet," she said, "Okay, level with me. Have you been drinking?"

I told her no, I had a virus, then said it several times just to hear how it sounded.

Ruth sighed loudly and said, "I don't know how your mother puts up with it."

I said again that I had a virus, prompting fake-Aunt Ruth to place a hand on my knee. "Honey," she said, squeezing it, "I didn't mean to upset you. I'm sorry, and if you're a little under the weather the first week at school, well, don't worry. It shouldn't be all that demanding. Now," she chirped, starting the car, "as soon as you feel better I'll get you pizza. Everything on it—you pick the place."

Vomit crawled up my throat but I vowed to ignore it. Nothing, I had decided, would prevent me from leaving. I would have my pizza. Then, like my fake-cousin Donnie, I would be off "to university."

The following week, Steve returned from New Jersey so that we could take a picnic out to the Hamptons—*The end-*

of-summer bash I have dreamed about for months, I wrote to my diary. *If only,* I added, *there wasn't this black cloud . . .* but there I stopped. The word *black* reminded me that I had a new black one-piece bathing suit. I put it on and stood in front of the mirror, admiring the straight smooth line it cut from breast to hip. As we pulled out of my driveway I asked Steve if he thought that I looked thin. Steve surveyed my body and said, "Yeah." Turning onto Sunrise, he added, "So did you get a blood test yet or what?"

I was shocked to hear someone else mention this. It made it seem real, like something suspected, then confirmed on the six o'clock news. I sat there. One minute passed. I said, "What?"

Steve sighed. "I said, you said on the phone last week your period was late. So did you get a blood test?"

I did not remember telling Steve that my period was late. I could not imagine exactly how I would have said it, since I had never actually said the words out loud. I sat there moving my lips, thinking, until he punched me in the arm and I blurted, "Okay, Steve. I will get the test. I'm sorry. It's just that I'm very nervous. And Dr. Leonard said it was not, you know, unlikely not to get it when things in life are changing. And that's what this is, Steve: a big change. Oh, Steve, it's really so very, very exciting. But I know I will love my new life. And you will, in time, come to love yours. It's truly time to move on. I'm sure it will work out. I just know—"

"So, you're saying," Steve interrupted, "that you didn't get the test because some doctor said you're nervous?"

"That's right, Steve. What do you know about it, anyway?"

He pulled over. "I know missing your period can mean you're pregnant."

I was shaking. I wanted to rip at his hair or possibly punch his face. Instead I said, "I'm sick to death of you ruining every day of my life. And I won't have you ruin this one. No way. I'm leaving—everything, mostly you and repressive, anti-intellectual Massapequa values. And that's it."

We were driving again. Steve had his hand raised in the stop sign. "Okay, just cool it," he said. "We're going on a picnic—a special day, like whatever it is you have in your family. So come on, just stop crying. We can talk about it later."

I got out of the car after two hours to see miles of sand separating the dunes from the water. Steve ran ahead of me, shouting over his shoulder, "It helps, asshole, if you pick the blanket up while you're walking." The blanket was a mess, I could see that, but my knees hurt and I was afraid that if I stopped I might drop it or fall. I felt slightly dizzy, my elbows ached. Perhaps, I thought, I had become like the ancient peasant women who, through the pains in their joints, can predict the future, or at least the weather. It would stay hot, I sensed. And something very definitely was going to happen. I thought of my mother and felt like crying. When at last I got to the spot where Steve had thrown his T-shirt, I was crying. I watched him go under a wave.

I said out loud, "You will make the sandwiches. Peanut butter. Liverwurst and tuna fish." But I was sweating. Steve's head popped up from a wave. I picked up the knife and ran it across the back of my wrist: I wanted to see blood. I was watching it drip onto a slice of white bread when Steve came out. He looked at my hand, then at my face. He said, "What the *fuck* is going on with you?"

My voice broke as I said, "It was an accident."

At home that night I lay awake, writing every few hours in my diary about how I wasn't having "the final daze"—with Steve or my friends—that I had hoped for. I reviewed possible explanations and would get through about ten before "being pregnant" bobbed up, like a newly tossed beer can in a canal. It seemed impossible: I didn't *look* pregnant. And there were explanations, related to tension, for missing a period. It seemed most impossible at this late date to involve others. "Just when things were going so well," my parents would shout. They might decide I could not leave for school! I came back to asking: What could I, without even a checking account, do on my own? There was no choice, it seemed, but to lie.

At 8:00 the next morning I called Steve. I told him that I'd had the test and that it had proved negative. Steve didn't ask how I'd been able to do it so quickly. He simply agreed that it was great. "Now," I told him, "I can enjoy my final days in this life. At last I can see all my friends to say goodbye."

He said, "You can see me. Your friends, for the hell of it, went up to the Poconos last night with Victor, Val's boyfriend. If you ever bothered to go out, you'd know." I hung up the phone and walked with my head down to my room. Taking a deep breath, sucking in my stomach all the way, I began to place the toiletries—the cold cream and tampons and Band-Aids—into my red flowered suitcase. Gwyn came in to help. My mother stood at the door with Sashi, smiling.

I left for college August 28 with my parents, my sisters and Coco, who slept on the top of my suitcase. I carried with me my purse and diary, along with a postcard of a girl in a bikini that I had received from my friends. They had *gone to Pocono, as a joke, from a bar, and got trapped by a storm, and missed you. Oh well!* Caro wished me luck. She said she'd call. *No lezzy stuff,* Val wrote at the bottom, *but, ya know, love and luck.*

After eight hours we arrived in Calverton, a small turn-of-the-century town situated in the middle of vineyards twenty-five miles southwest of Rochester. I had no idea what I was supposed to do. Standing, sweating, outside my dorm, I felt as I had left alone on catechism day. My mother hugged me and said, "Don't be discouraged. No one in the family has ever gone off to college before, and it's bound to be a little scary at first. But there's absolutely nothing to be afraid of, sweetheart. It can only get easier." They stood there with me a while longer, then got into the car and drove home.

Inside my room Christina Cutrone, a large-boned Westchester girl with a black Farrah Fawcett shag, was sifting pot on top of a New Riders album. She had an entire shoe box filled with Hawaiian. She had set up her prom pictures alongside it. "Hey roomie," she said, snorting a roach, "welcome to your new life at Old Cal."

I wrote home almost immediately, describing the old red brick buildings, the modern cement walkways and the dorms, explaining how they were arranged into suites, tiny three-room corridors connected to private living rooms. I wrote in another letter about my suitemates—Laroo Pollack, a junior Sociology major with a perm who on our first night had announced, "I can live with frosh, but if you play heavy metal, if you do hard drugs, I will be forced to call security"; her roommate, Sarie Reinhardt, a thin, stringy blonde who smoked brown cigarettes and wore Hare Krishna dresses with Frye boots; and, in the single room, a fat farm girl named Suzi Butkes, who, like an old lady in a movie theater, paraphrased what people said right after they said it.

I enjoyed spending time with these girls—loved walking in a clump back to campus late Saturday night, then filing out Sunday noon, late for brunch. But I loved to be without them just as much. While they set up backgammon boards and planned keg parties, I was out practicing my flute, in the library, at a lecture or arriving early for class to review the notes I'd copy over in my room before dinner. With the exception of Laroo, my suitemates had come to Calverton "to party down." I had come—I'd tell anyone who asked—to change my life, which was why in my spare time I followed around this black-haired hippie guy, a mysterious man as different physically from Steve as one could be.

Spotting him by a coffee machine, I'd push a bandanna down to my eyebrows in the hopes I'd appear more countercultural. Spotting him later at dinner, at a table with olive-skinned men who wore blue-and-white shawls around their shoulders, I'd push it so low I could not see. One night the guy walked over to our table and gave me a book—*Revolution for the Hell of It* by Abbie Hoffman—then walked off. Alongside a photo of kids at a protest, he'd written in the tiniest writing I'd ever seen, *This could have been you.*

"Weird-o," said Christina, putting a cigarette out in her mashed potatoes and stirring. "If he talks to you again," Laroo said, pointing her fork, "you call security."

I nodded and watched him glide off, hands behind his back, head lifted, as if he were out observing nature.

The next day he appeared in the hall by Humanities A. He told me that his name was Dhani, pronounced "Donny," that I would never be able to pronounce his last name; it was foreign, although he did not say from what country. I was so excited by this I could not sleep. As Christina snored, I'd write about how *strangely erotic* I felt, about my *strangely large breasts—intense and ready for action!*

The weather remained warm through the second week of school, and on my eighteenth birthday I walked with Dhani along a stream that ran through the vineyards. He told me that the fascist Erie Dining Hall would not serve brown rice. Nodding, I took my shirt off to impress him and spread out on a rock in the sun. "Hey," Dhani said, hugging himself. "It's not *that* warm." But I was eighteen now, a new person who was free, and did not care.

The next morning Dhani rolled over and asked, "You're on the pill, right?"

Scrambling up, I said no, that I timed it in my head.

He asked me if I was kidding. I shook my head and he said, "So how do you know that you aren't pregnant right now? You could be pregnant this very second and not know it."

"Shut up, Dhani," I replied, gathering my clothes. "Don't talk to me this way."

"Calm down," he said, leaning up on one elbow. "It is a reasonable thing to ask. I'll ask now only that you think about it. Fair?"

"Well, you have a lot of nerve telling me what to do," I said as I put my pants on backward.

When I got close to my dorm I stopped running. I turned my face up into early sun. I said, "Everything is beautiful. There is work. Sex with Dhani is so creative!" Ignoring the way my voice cracked, I told myself that I would eventually use the ten boxes of tampons I'd bought one day with Gwyn. It was a matter of time.

FIVE

In western New York everyone tells the same joke about the snow—how if you're lucky it starts in August and how if you're lucky it ends in August. By mid-September I had heard this line easily 500 times, most often from Suzi Butkes, who repeated it with the insider's glee I had once felt telling Gwyn, "You're in *big* trouble." I noted the signs: long down coats and mittens on the girls who wore lockets and sweaters; bulky army-style jackets on the ponytailed guys who lived off-campus. Dhani, in lotus position on his bamboo meditation mat, lightly shivered. Christina, wrapped in blankets, failed to get up before noon. But I felt fine — running to class in sweaters that pressed my "strangely large" breasts flat and low; sitting by open windows to read *Middlemarch*. If anything I was sort of sweaty, due, I wrote, *to my excitement about life, to my new sexual-intellectual power.*

On September 20, however, I woke up shaking. My pink quilt was on the floor; something wet seemed to be on my face. I thought that perhaps my plant had spilled, but what I saw as I turned was snow.

I sat cross-legged on my bed and stared out. Unlike any snow I'd ever seen, this didn't seem to consist of individual flakes. It was frenzied, a blizzardy disarray blowing so fast and so violently, it formed a wall. "Close the window, for Christ's sake," Christina mumbled, her head raised half an inch off the pillow. "What are you, stoned?"

Actually I felt kind of stoned. When I closed my eyes I saw white; when I opened them, objects in the room looked bleached, as after a photoflash. "I'm sorry," I said, moving one hand along the sheet toward the window, "I feel kind of spaced." But Christina had gone back to her snoring. I looked out a few minutes more at the snow. Then I walked nervously into the bathroom as I had each morning for two months, sure that my period would have come in the night. And at last that day of the storm I saw red!

I studied the smudge as I might have a microscope specimen. I stretched the crotch of my underwear in all directions to get a better view. I brought my nose within one inch. I concluded from this position that the mark was not menstrual blood; it was the pattern, a field of red strawberries, showing through against white cotton. Letting my head drop against the stall door, I reviewed a list I'd made the day before of All the Great Things in Life That Await Me—a synopsis of a future so wonderful, there could not possibly be anything wrong with my life now.

I began with Dhani, who was teaching me Kundalini yoga, which I would master by the time I saw my family at Winter Festival. There were new friendships to develop and challenging schoolwork, but there was also, superimposed on this list, a black spot, a blot like the stains broken Bics had left in high school pockets. Without naming the problem, I said, It's your great first semester, nothing will happen, the same way I'd said in July, This will end because you are leaving. It was late September, the top snap of my carpenter's pants flapped open like a tiny collar, and it seemed clear that nothing had ended. But I made myself stop. All around me blow-dryers clicked on like cars gunning their engines before a race. I stood and walked with my suitemates out through the storm to get breakfast.

On line at Erie Dining Hall, I said to myself, You feel fine. But the food, as we moved closer, smelled kind of strange, like milk left in the sun or rancid butter. My forehead felt hot. There was an odd tingling in one breast. My hands were shaking—so badly that as I walked out into the hall I dropped my tray. The room erupted with cheers and clapping. Laroo said, "Nice one," Big Suzi laughed as, stunned, I stepped over folds of French toast, a puddle of juice, and sat down alongside Christina. Casually I tried to watch my suitemates eat. Laroo, keeping one eye on me, licked the rim of her toast. Big Suzi guzzled juice to keep from giggling, while Christina stabbed an egg. I stared as the yellow fluid swam onto her plate, the substance that might ooze out, I thought, if you stabbed Barbie. "Excuse me, please," I said as I stood up. And then I ran. Laroo shouted something about cocaine. Christina, calling, "Wait," jogged behind me.

When I'd thought of something to tell her, I slowed down. I said, "I'm probably just exhausted. I've been studying so hard. I'll go back to the room for a while and rest. I'll be fine."

"Okay, roomie," Christina said, the blood of Barbie cracked on her lips. "I'll bring you a roll."

Unzipping the carpenter's pants one inch, I said thanks.

Back in my room the dizziness passed. "Perhaps you've had a quick flu," I said out loud, "a virus due to a cold." Whatever it was had left an aftershock, the kind of giddy pulse I'd felt before on speed, the kind calmed only by sex or by cigarettes smoked quickly. I lit a cigarette and put it out. I called Dhani. There was no answer. I paced. Then, passing Christina's desk, I knew what I felt like doing: I wanted more than anything to steal.

I had stolen with other girls when I was younger, walked out of stores with peace-sign stickers or metallic silver studs, once with a pair of blue corduroy bell-bottoms I'd given to Caro. Now, I reminded myself, I was an A student in college. I had thick books with small type and a boyfriend who deemed owning more than one sweater an indication of "aspiritual values." But all of this did not seem to matter. I was vibrating as I watched the desk, the impulse to look inside as strong, I imagined, as the one boys suddenly had to drop what they were doing, then to masturbate. One second later my hand was on Christina's drawer. Opening it, I saw a square silver earring missing a pearl, a necklace made of pink shells, a five-dollar bill and a wooden coin. I gathered the objects and wrapped them in one of my "grown-up lady" hankies. Then I stuffed the bundle deep inside my dresser drawer.

Standing there I said, "You will study," picked up one book and put it down. I flipped through record albums. I lit and stamped out three cigarettes, then got on hands and knees and, from the edge of the bed, watched the snow, which seemed to come harder, as if a stagehand had dumped the flakes marked "snow scene" all at once. But the glare was so strong I looked away: at the rug I had knitted by hand, at Christina's "Cats of the World" calendar, at the phone. After playing a while with the cord, I dialed the campus operator and asked for the birth-control clinic number. It will be closed, I said to myself as I dialed, due to snow, but at least you can say that you tried. I inhaled and said this again—at least you tried—and found myself thinking about the Bill place and my mother, and then suddenly a high voice like Sarie Reinhardt's said, "Birth Control Information Center, how may I help you?" Things in the room blurred white with the light of the snow. I had no idea what to say. I dropped the receiver.

I looked around for something to kick, for some way, as Dhani would say, to reshape the energy expended in crying by transferring it onto an object. Nothing presented itself. I ran through the List of Things That Await Me and, calmed by that, opened *Middlemarch* to the long paragraph I'd been on for two days. I decided to give myself another two days with it and called Dhani, who was, according to his roommate, "out somewhere digging the snow." The roommate told me not to cry. He said that I was wrong, that it would someday stop snowing. In the meantime, he said, he was there, "ready and available in place of Big Don." I said no thanks, no message, and hung up, lighting another cigarette.

The first week of October, I noticed a lump the size of a softball lodged in the lower half of my waist. When Christina left the room I'd pull a chair to the dresser, stand on it and stare into the mirror. Sucking in my stomach so that the ribs showed, I'd turn in a circle, become dizzy and fall off. I'd do sit-ups, I'd run up and down to the laundry room, jog through several suites, then climb back onto the chair. Finding the lump unchanged, I'd start to talk: There were things to look forward to, I'd say, wonderful things so rightfully mine it seemed impossible some other nameless thing might interfere. Besides, in practical terms, none of my friends had noticed a change, which suggested that there hadn't been one. And, I thought, should a slight change take place I could, like Suzi Butkes, simply dress in the bathroom. Putting Calverton sweatshirts over pants that gapped at the zipper, I'd walk to class reciting the List of Great Things That Await Me. I'd say, quoting Dhani, Be here now. But the lump remained.

On October 8 I put on a pair of jeans and saw each tooth of zipper exposed. On the tenth I put on another pair and found the zipper stopped halfway. For days after, I'd run to class, come home, stand on the chair, fall off, then run out again, staring at other waists as I'd once gazed at Val's go-go boots. I did not say, You are pregnant. I said, out loud as I ran, "There is time. This will pass."

On the morning of October 15, I woke up, said, "This will pass. There is time," ran into the bathroom and threw up. It was the flu, I told myself—dating from the winter before, the summer, and September 20. I counted my breaths, one at a time, to keep from crying. Reaching eleven, I inhaled, raised one hand and slapped the stomach: It was hard! I slapped it again as if executing an illegal hit in volleyball and watched the bathroom tile blur to white, as things had the day of the storm, which reminded me that another storm was on its way. Lowering my hand, I searched for things to say. I tried reciting one of the lists. Giving that up, I said to myself, You had a cyst under your arm in eleventh grade and it looked this way. Christina called.

"Hey, roomie," she was shouting. "What's going on? You have a letter." In the distance Laroo yelled, "Is she out?" I said, "I have my period." Christina shouted "She has her period" at Suzi, who reported to Laroo, "It's not cocaine."

I took my letter, said to Laroo, through Suzi, "I'm not doing cocaine," and walked out by myself to the living room. The letter was from Steve. He wanted to visit Calverton or to have me visit him. I did not want to see Steve. I could not imagine what we'd find to discuss. I put the letter down and lit a cigarette. Letting smoke leak slowly from my nostrils, I watched students struggle home through the snow. I thought of something I could tell myself. It was this: The snow made us all look bad. It was hard, it seemed, even on a good day to keep your balance.

I had received other letters. Caro and Val had written, forgetting usually to sign their names. My parents wrote almost daily. My father drew our childhood cartoon creatures on the envelope. My mother "definitely sympathized" with my suddenly having no time to write; it always seemed to have taken her *"two whole days* to get this one off" to me—this along with the foil-wrapped cookies, the articles clipped from *The New York Times* or *Massapequa Post,* plus the little felt-and-sparkle pillows Sashi made "to go on your collage bed. Soon you have a whole set!"

And there were letters from my grandparents. My grandfather wrote of his college years in Ohio. Nanny Florita told of finding truth in Christian Science, while Nanny Etta remained ever hopeful that my new locale would at last move me in the direction of Orthodox Judaism. She prayed for this daily. Since it went without saying that I was not eating well, she counseled me to keep on hand "a can of Bumble Bee tuna, fresh eggs, milk—whole only—cheese and cake (Entenmann's). . . ." If nothing else, I was to be sure to remember that "A nice little snack of Tam Tams and jam is always nourishing." She sent books: One week it was Bible stories for young adults, another, a novel called *Elyza,* "a clean, wholesome story of a fine, clean young Jewish woman that you, number-one girl, will find very fulfilling." There was always a check for ten dollars because "a young lady should always have something in her purse." And oh, yes, she'd emphasize in her P.S., whatever I did I was not "under any circumstances to go out into that snow."

By mid-October I felt as if it had been snowing for a year, although it had been snowing only one month and I had been at school for barely two. The sidewalks in town looked like strips of frozen lake, deep yellow ponds you could look down inside of, expecting still silver-eyed fish to stare back. The smells of wet down and sweaty flannel hung in the air, thick as soup. Classrooms were chilly and there were rarely dry seats, or else the seats were so tight I'd have to sit sideways —an odd condition I attributed vaguely, like all else, to the snow. I felt depressed. I mentioned this one day to Christina.

My roommate, looking behind her bed for the shell necklace, said, "Cool out. Everyone is depressed. My Social Psych prof said 'The winter months have a depressive effect on the individual psyche.'" I asked Christina when she thought it would stop. Sounding annoyed, she said, "How the hell should I know? Are you sure you haven't seen my necklace?" I coughed, said no and walked into the bathroom. Laroo followed. Turning on the water, she asked, "Have you put on weight?" I stiffened, said, "No, I'm fine," and walked out. Laroo, imitating Steve Martin, called, "Excuuuse me." As I entered the room Christina whined, "Where the fuck is it?" I said, "I don't know," and lay down on the bed as the window flew up and blizzard warnings, stapled to a bulletin board in the hall, flapped in sudden wind.

The next big storm hit on Halloween. Classes were canceled and I stayed in bed reading as my suitemates prepared for a party somewhere downtown. Three of them stood in the door to show me their costumes. Then Laroo, shouting, "Da-da-dah," pushed through into the room wearing curlers and a bathrobe, beneath which she'd stuffed a pillow. She was going as a pregnant housewife. I stared at her, not knowing if this was a joke or a comment or a coincidence, or whether I should be wondering any of this, as I was, officially, fine. She threw a pencil at me. "Why aren't you coming?" she asked. I stammered, then said that I had work and that later on I might see Dhani, although Dhani seemed to have vanished. "Good," she said, ramming her pillow-belly into Christina, "you need it," and one by one they left.

I sat at the edge of my bed reading "Heart of Darkness." Next I read a ditto on Bronze Age tools. When ten minutes had passed I opened my desk drawer and pulled out *Our Bodies, Ourselves,* a book I had stolen from Sarie one day while she was in the shower. It was my habit to casually flip through the parts on rape and lesbians, study the pictures relating to sex, then move on to the line drawings labeled "Stages of Pregnancy." Standing on my chair, Halloween, I looked at the image in the mirror, then closely at the "second trimester" woman on the page. But trying to make my mouth move, to make myself say, You are pregnant and must do something, I seemed to freeze.

I could, on any day, stare at the lump, now the size of a deflated basketball, for ten minutes or an hour without result. I could see myself clearly enough—a girl standing on a chair, her pants open, her sweatshirt raised—but it was like looking at a picture of yourself from a year or two before: Something slight had changed, the hair perhaps or the eyebrows, but it was hard to say what. Inevitably I'd feel dizzy and stop, or someone would knock. I'd have a class. On Halloween the phone rang. It was Steve.

"Just seein' if you're still alive," he said. "So, why don't you come to my school? The weather ain't as bad." I looked around my room. The sheets had not been changed in weeks. Snow was piled in my plants like a frothy white fungus. "Okay, Steve," I said, "I'll come."

I left the following Friday, stealing a ten-dollar bill and a silver-and-turquoise ring from my roommate, who walked me, tight-lipped, to the bus. "Now, have a good time," she said, forcing a smile, "do everything I would do." Christina, I thought as I sat down, seemed unfriendly: I had woken lately to find her gone. Coming in after class, I'd hear her whispering with Suzi in Laroo's room. I thought about her shell necklace, but as if thinking about my body, said, Stop. I had reading to do. I had to pee and maneuvered my way to the back of the bus, only to find I didn't have to. I thought again of Laroo, who had cystitis, then changed the subject to food. I was hungry. Walking back to my seat, I thought about having dinner with Steve. It would actually be good to eat with Steve, to eat anywhere else, to relax and stop these thoughts, which seemed to spill, one linked to the next, circling, accumulating like a chain letter lost in the brain.

The first thing Steve did was to pull open the white ski coat I kept half-zippered. He said, "You gained weight." After he'd snapped his fingers beneath my nose I denied it, and he said, messing up my hair, that it was fine. "It happens," he said, "you know, you eat that shit SUNY food. Anyway, it looks cute—this little ball—typical cute antics."

Later that night Steve seemed to change his mind. We'd been having sex in his dorm room—the lights off at my request—when casually he ran a hand across my stomach. I felt the hand stop. He turned on the light. He said, "Are you pregnant?"

I sat up and said, "What are you talking about? I just gained weight."

"Well," Steve said, his voice louder, "it's just that it's not, you know, like a normal way to gain weight. It's all smushed into this one part. And it's like bone or something. It's not like fat."

I was standing on the other side of the room at this point. "Steve," I said, "please don't insult me. I had that test. You know it. So why are you doing this to me? You're trying to scare me, to exert dominant male control. I control my own body and my destiny."

Steve sat up. "Cool new language, huh? Well, Miss Woman's Libber, I'll just let you worry about it, since it's your destiny."

I was tempted to tell Steve about Dhani, about how strangely erotic I had been, about how Dhani did not eat innocent animals for food. Instead, feeling dizzy, I said, "I'm hungry."

Steve said, "But we had dinner and dessert, and snacks and popcorn." I took a deep breath and shouted, "I'm hungry, goddammit. I'm hungry." Someone knocked and said, "Okay in there?" Steve said, "Yeah, fine," and I dressed quickly in a corner, then walked out behind him to the Union. There, at 2:00 A.M., I ate a deluxe submarine sandwich with four kinds of meat and vegetables, half a bag of shredded lettuce, one-quarter pound of Swiss cheese, seven tomatoes and four tablespoons of mayonnaise. I washed it down with orange and cream soda, then walked home with the hiccups.

"I guess the weather's getting to you," Steve said Sunday as he put me on the Rochester bus. I told him that things were fine. From my seat, I waved and tried to laugh. Then the bus pulled out and I stared at Convenient stores, at the houses with weather vanes, the tractors with snow on the seats, then at the miles of gnarled stringy vineyard. Somewhere in the middle of it the bus pulled off the road.

Harsh overhead bulbs snapped on and passengers groaned. "This'll only take a minute," growled the driver as he walked like John Wayne to the rear. My stomach was whining in time with long ribbons of sweat exiting my armpits. It seemed the driver was looking at me. It seemed for some reason that he planned to throw me off the bus. By the time he reached my seat, on his way only to the bathroom in back, I was in tears, my face buried in my coat so that he'd have a harder time finding me.

When I returned it was November 3 and close to midterms. My suitemates got up early, packed their knapsacks and hurried out to the library. Christina studied on her bed, lighting joints, speaking only if I asked her questions. On the cover of a notebook I analyzed it this way: *We are all in our separate spheres, preparing for big tests, which gives me some relief.* Placing a sweatshirt and bathrobe over pants halfway open at the zipper, I'd say, "See ya later." Christina would nod and I'd walk, one hand on the wall, to the study room downstairs.

Seated at a carrel far from the door, I sorted through the Cycladic Islanders and Assyrians for Western Civ. I translated half of "Un Coeur Simple" for French Literature of the Nineteenth Century and completed the Literature of the Victorian Era, Britain take-home test. Then I came to Philosophy 101. I could get through the three arguments that proved God's existence. I could fill in truth tables. But anytime I tried to study free will, my eyes would wander off the page, past the footnotes to the strained buttons of my bathrobe. I'd try to make a joke. "The Blob," I would murmur, "the blob," until someone else would say, "Shut up." Standing, I'd attempt sucking in the blob, give up, and walk quickly to a bathroom off the lobby.

Every day during midterms it was something new.

One day there'd be a rippling motion beneath the blob; on another, streaky red lines across it to suggest a map showing patterns of migration. I'd race through lists, reassurances, probabilities like an analysand on speed. But nothing worked — not the idea of time remaining, not a cyst, not stress, not the life I was destined to have. I'd end up saying: It, this, has not passed. What's passed is time, suggesting that soon someone, some girl, might notice. I dreaded this. At the same time, I sensed that someone knowing could not be worse than my hiding, even though I still could not make myself say what from, or what would happen if someone found me out—I had to stop! I had exams and papers, and so I'd go back to my books, no conclusions reached about free will, about my situation or Dhani, who had disappeared, or about Christina, who slammed doors.

Midterms passed and it continued to snow. Two of my professors told me how pleased they were with my essays. Christina said, "I can't believe what a fucking pigsty mess this room is," took her knapsack and walked out. Everyone else said only, "Have a great Thanksgiving break. See ya at the end of the semester."

The student bus service left for Long Island November 20. The front seats were occupied by the lockets-and-sweaters crew, the backseats, near me, by the ten-years-too-late set— the straggly-haired girls in overalls, the guys with the guitars and wire-rimmed glasses. Ten minutes onto the Thruway, one of them began to bark his way through "Just Like a Woman" and, "for the more boo-jois among us," Simon and Garfunkel standards—"America," "Homeward Bound"—hoping to excite us into believing we were on our way to a march or a protest and not Long Island.

I sang along with my seatmate, a peroxide blonde from Wantagh named Donna who didn't really know the lyrics. When the songs ended, after one of the guys with round glasses had cheered, "Right on, bro," there were still eight hours to go. Nine hours after that, near 6:00 P.M., we saw the Empire State Building, and at 7:30 pulled finally into Hempstead. From Donna's window I saw Steve walking in a circle to keep warm. I remembered that something was wrong, but immediately forgot what. "It was nice sitting with you," Donna said, turning to face me, "I guess I'll go." I was exhausted. I could not move. "Well, I guess I'll go," said Donna. Still I sat there. She called my name. She nudged me, and very slowly I lifted up from my seat and walked off.

Steve seemed startled by my appearance, his mouth and eyes pulsing rhythmically as if his face were a large, fleshy vent. We stood there staring at each other. At last Steve moved his lips and said, "Hi ya." After another minute had passed he told me that the old gang was "keepin' the beer cold" at some new bar. "I don't care," I said, "please take me home." Steve got his face under control and said, "Fine." In the car I immediately pretended to fall asleep. Twenty minutes later we were there. Coco was barking. My father was at the door. "Thank you, sir," he said to Steve as he took my suitcase. I wanted to say something to Steve—I had, after all, said nothing—but my father closed the door on his face. I was inside.

Sashi was jumping in front of me, talking: Gwyn, she said, was out with her new boyfriend, Rick; my mother would be back in a minute from ballet class; Coco had gotten a shot and was sleepy. She stood there smiling and I smiled back. My father, also smiling, said, "Take off your jacket—stay a while." Sashi said, "Yeah, aren't you hot?" I said, "Me? I'm totally fine," and walked into the kitchen, wiggling out of my ski coat. Walking back out, I folded one arm across the blob and handed the coat to my sister.

Sashi looked at my face, then at my stomach, but seemed to see only her oldest sister, home intact from college. Skipping to the hall closet for a hanger, she said, "What time do you get up at school? What do you eat at school?" I opened my mouth to answer, but my father, standing by the door, spoke first. "Looks as if those starches have dug in a bit, old girl," he said, no longer smiling. Sashi returned and pulled me into the living room. To my father I said, "Oh, Dad." To Sashi I said, "We eat in the fascist Erie Dining Hall, where they will not serve brown rice."

"How come?" she asked as we sat on the couch. I was repeating random phrases I had heard from Dhani—"proteins based in beans and sorghum"; "institutional mistreatment of animals"—when my father joined us. He sat down across from me and stared. "They don't consider seaweed a viable foodstuff," I announced.

"So," he said, "do you manage to get any exercise with all the snow?"

"Dad," I said, "my whole life changes, and you ask about exercise?"

He lit his pipe. Sashi said, "Don't you want to call all your friends?" I had not really thought about this. I did not want to think about it. "Which ones do you mean?" I asked, but my father interrupted, wishing to discuss French literature of the nineteenth century. Sashi said, "You know, like Vally and Caro and Steve, like your friends." My father spoke in a loud voice about Gustave Flaubert *et le mot juste.* The conversation was getting confused. I was relieved to hear my mother approaching the door.

"Look at my big girl," she said, tossing her dance bag aside to hug me. "You look wonderful." I turned to sneer at my father, who stood and stretched. "Looks as if we've gained a little weight," he said, "but nothing serious, we'll hope." My mother looked at him and faked an exasperated sigh. "Honey," she told him, smiling at me, "now's not the time to worry about waistlines. It's a holiday! We'll worry about that after the New Year. Now," she said, leading me back to the kitchen, "we have your dinner all ready on a plate in the refrigerator, and you must sit in your chair and tell us every last detail."

By midnight I had gotten up to the events of early October. It was invigorating to think of school solely in terms of books and projects and outings. Still I was exhausted. My head practically lay on my plate. My mother winked at my father and led me upstairs. "Welcome home, sweetheart," she said as she closed my door. "Goodnight, babe," my father called. I heard the murmur of my parents' voices, my father's slightly excited. I said, You are home, and fell asleep.

I slept until noon the next day and woke up in a sweat. Walking into the kitchen, I announced, "I didn't mean to sleep so late. I'm sorry."

Gwyn was talking on the phone as she reviewed a piano score with an emery board. Cupping the receiver, she whispered, "Welcome home. You're allowed to sleep."

I felt confused. I wasn't sure, standing there, if I was supposed to kiss Gwyn. I hadn't seen her in months—according to the calendar on the refrigerator, almost three. But coming in this way to find her sitting by the phone, in so familiar a scene, I wondered for a second if I'd really been gone.

Gwyn hung up the phone. "Sweedhawt," she said, imitating a great-aunt. "Welcome back to the Planet Mommy and Daddy. The Planet Mom left some coffee with a note." I looked at the note. It said, *Relax. You are home!!!* There was a smile face. I stared at it for a minute, then looked back at

Gwyn, who had her eyes on my stomach. "So," she said, "I guess you gained a little weight."

"Well," I said, certain that I *had* been gone, "maybe a little." And I began to talk about the starch-heavy food, about Dhani and my dorm. My sister smiled and nodded. She asked me questions. She seemed to have noticed something odd. But I was her older sister. If I said I was fine or acted fine, I was fine; like Sashi and my mother, she would naturally give me the benefit of the doubt.

Later that afternoon I put my father's coat over a sweatshirt and a pair of sweatpants and walked over to Caro's hardware store, Carlucci's. I was so excited about seeing her, I tripped and fell on my way in. The owner, who sold fishing bait to my father, stood behind the counter and watched me. "Is Carolynne Carroway here?" I asked, standing up. The man lifted his eyes to my face, shook his head and pointed to Caro, who was playing with keys at his side.

"Space is the place," she said, hopping the counter. "God, Rainbo and me waited at the bar all night for you last night. Too smart for us, huh? Just kiddin'. So, God, I thought you'd never get home. Same old shit, only more around here. So, how are you?" I smiled so hard my lips ached from the effort. I talked about my dorm, about the superiority of brown rice, but Caro, who'd glanced quickly at my stomach as you might a man's crotch, had stopped smiling. "So," she said, her bottom lip visibly wiggling, "I, uh, really have to get back to work." She nodded at her boss. "But, let's see . . . I'll, well, I'll talk to you soon." Turning her back to me, she walked off. I stood there for a minute face to face with the owner, who was still staring. Caro at his side distractedly fingered keys. I felt like shaking her, screaming, "Come on, it's *me*," but I turned and left, feeling more nervous than I had when I'd come in.

I was scheduled to be home eight days and began that

night to make phone calls, attempting to set up some dates. I left messages at Val's and at Caro's, hoping their mothers would tell them how educated and interesting I now sounded. I called Rainbo but hung up when Caro answered. I called Steve, who said, "So, did you talk to any of your friends? What did they say to you?" During the day I read and watched TV; at night I stayed in with my sisters to read and watch TV. I went to bed early, upset by the fact that I was not having all the great fun that had awaited me.

Two days after I saw Caro, Val called. She'd be too busy to get together, she explained, because Victor had rented them a ranch-style house in downtown Lindenhurst. She'd already heard, though, how much I loved school; she'd heard too that I'd gained weight. "You know what people look at," she said as I denied it. "They could care less you get good grades. If you don't keep up the old appearance, well, you know."

That night, Caro came by with two younger girls I'd never seen before. We sat in my room, sorting through the hundreds of pictures I had taken of my campus. Caro, who would not look directly at me, chain-smoked six cigarettes. The two girls on my bed exchanged glances. I started talking faster and louder. Caro finally stood midsentence and said, "I have to be at work early," punched me lightly on the arm and wandered out with her head down. "Have a great break," the two girls said as they followed.

With the exception of my parents, no one on my "great break" had managed to sustain a full conversation with me. All exchanges were brief and cryptic, laced, I was certain, with innuendo. On the twenty-sixth I wrote, *The thought of one more person acting cold, like the glass-eyed pods in Invasion of the Body Snatchers, makes me want to throw up more than I already have to.* But I could not go on to write more, to ask why people seemed odd or why I felt sick. I was afraid at this late date to ask anything. Sitting in the beanbag chair, I considered the possibility that it was other people who had changed and not me: Val's remark could have reflected some new insight, an awareness of how false Massapequa values really were; Caro might have been bored and demoralized—a girl living at home past her time.

On the twenty-seventh, the night before I went back, I was no longer so eloquent. *What is wrong with these girls?* I wrote, had a spasm in my hand and dropped the pen.

Later, as I started to pack, my mother came into my room and closed the door. "Okay," she said, folding her arms, "there's something Daddy and I have to ask you about. We've waited, and now I have to ask you."

"What's that?" I asked, rolling up socks.

"Betsy Israel," she said, grabbing one sock, "are you pregnant?"

My body rattled like a pinball machine. "No, Mother," I managed to say, "I am not pregnant."

"Are you sure?"

"Yes, thank you, I am sure," I said, then added, to make it more convincing, "I mean, I just had one of those appointments with, uh, you know, with a gynecologist. Oh, Mother, it was gross." I was pleased with this. It sounded sincere and youthful, like something Betty, the girl in the menstruation movie, would have said to her mom.

"So what did he have to say about this belly?" my mother asked, scowling.

"Nothing, Mother. They said nothing. There was nothing to say. I'm fine."

"Well," she said, inhaling for a sigh, "maybe you should see another doctor. See what someone else says. I have to say, Betsy, I don't like the looks of this one bit."

"Mother, for Christ's sake, I told you I'm fine. I ate too much, that's all. Now I have to pack."

"Well," she said, still inhaling, "if you won't see a doctor, perhaps you should think about some serious exercise. I don't know—something to help take off some of this weight."

I slammed the red flowered suitcase. "What is this shit about weight?" I shouted. "Every person doesn't have to be a dancer rail, okay?"

She exhaled into her sigh. "Okay," she said, "I'm sorry. I certainly didn't intend to upset you. I'm just worried, that's my job—I'm your mother. But if you say you're all right . . . well, I don't know what to say. At least . . . well, I don't know." She sighed again and looked around. "Do you need any help packing?" she finally said. "Is there something you want me to iron?"

That night I couldn't sleep. I hauled out the List of Great Things That Await Me but got stuck after "family." I decided to review my life. I began by saying, In the five months and three weeks since the senior prom, my entire life has changed. I stopped. I felt cold and uncomfortable. The rippling sensation, a light, fluttery pressure beneath the skin, had returned. I sat up, hyperventilating, then tipped over and just lay there.

At around midnight Steve called, "too damned late," my father said as I grabbed the phone.

"I feel worried," Steve said. "You should get a physical."

"Steve," I said, "it is almost finals. I don't have time for physicals. Don't you understand that? How can you be so unreasonable? And Steve, just for the record, it's none of your goddamned business." Steve started to yell and I hung up the phone, walking past my father, who'd stood listening outside the kitchen and now followed me with his eyes back up the stairs.

I was the first in the suite to return, and worked for a day on my clothes. I ripped open the waist seams on my carpenter's pants, then did the same to my oldest jeans, accidentally tearing a huge slash down the thigh. Throwing them out, I cut my pink Calverton sweatshirt up the sides, then cut a sweater I'd stolen from Gwyn, who had looked thin. I was stretching a girdle out over my head as Christina walked in, threw down her knapsack, picked up her pot and walked out. I heard her mumbling across the hall in Laroo's room. I heard Laroo say, "From now on we keep the doors locked."

This scene, with slight variations, was replayed each day the first week of December: Christina would walk in, look in her drawers, then walk out across the hall to Laroo's. With Sarie and Suzi they'd leave for Erie without me. I'd consider running after them, but I was out of breath all the time. I could not imagine running. Nor could I imagine eating with them. The only clear wish I had was to be transported into the future or at least out of my body, away from them and back to the person I'd been. I'd read random paragraphs from my books or walk downstairs to the lobby, where I'd buy candy from the machines.

One early December night as I sat eating peanut M & M's, the phone rang. I was startled: The phone had not rung in days. Suspiciously I picked it up. "Hello, my little friend," said Dhani. "How have you been?" I said that I'd been great, and Dhani said that he'd been busy with "political work of a complicated nature," but that now he had free time. "When you catch your breath," he said, "come over for a holiday visit." It was the first time since Thanksgiving anyone had invited me anywhere. I said I'd come.

At Dhani's that afternoon, I closed my eyes and tried to attain lotus position on the bamboo meditation mat. Pretending to unzipper the pants already open, I said that I felt "strangely erotic." Dhani tried to roll on top of me. After a few minutes, however, he rolled off. "Your shape," he mumbled, waving his hand in an artistic S through the air, "has lost its essential proportions." I searched for a response but came up with nothing. Finally I said, "It's all those starches." Sitting up, I added, "My friends are waiting for me. I really have to get back."

On December 9 the dorm sponsored a formal holiday party. I laid out the slinky salmon gown I'd worn to my prom, recalling how glamorous I had looked that night, how even Jason had said so. But now, struggling with the zipper, I saw the blob jut out, firm and sure as a basketball. Steve, who'd driven up just for this night, saw it too. "Are you sure about not being pregnant?" he asked.

My arms went limp, all energy draining out through my fingertips as if vacuumed. Unable to move, I stood looking down at the shoes lined up neatly in my closet. I said to myself, There is time, but, counting my shoes, I knew there wasn't. Somehow, very soon, this situation—the very obvious fact that I was sick—would blow apart. I couldn't bear to imagine what that meant; what I'd have to do; what my parents would do; what Steve would do to me. I pictured blood and intestines. I pictured other things—not coming back to school; coming back and being asked by Laroo to leave the suite. I had to stop. I had six finals to get through, then Winter Festival. Even if time seemed to be shrinking, I had to continue.

We walked into the hall seconds later to discover that everyone had gone ahead without us. Finding our table at the dance, I saw that no places for us had been set. Big Suzi looked at me, passed a joint to Laroo and then snorted.

"Nice," Steve said, punching my arm a little too hard. "Glad to see you got as many friends here as you got at home."

When I did not argue this point, Steve touched my

shoulder. "Hey," he said, "I'm sorry." He placed my arm around his waist. But my hand slid down the back of his jacket as if it were oiled. I couldn't keep it up.

A few days later Christina flung open our door so hard it hit the wall. She threw down her knapsack and started banging things around her side of the room.

From the bed I asked, "What's going on?"

"What's going on?" she said, turning to face me. "What's going on? This," she said, pulling the shell necklace from a pants pocket, "is what's going on." She waved it in the air and opened her mouth. "I found this in your drawer. I had to get proof. You asshole. Asshole! How dare you—"

"Christina," I said, sitting up. "What are you talking about? I might have borrowed it sometime. I don't remember—"

"Fuck you," she snapped. "I've had it with you. Don't give me that shit. I thought you were smart. I thought you were a good kid. I couldn't believe it was you, even though Roo figured you out right away." She was standing over the bed, her arms folded, her eyes narrowed to the black slits Chinese people in cartoons have for eyes. "What are you going to say?" she demanded, "Why did you do it?" She was shouting. "Say something."

"I don't know what you're talking about," I tried, "I must have borrowed it and forgot . . ."

Christina dropped the necklace onto my body. "You," she said, walking out, "are an asshole."

After Laroo's door had slammed I got up, tried to zipper my coat, gave up and walked quickly down the stairs to the back door. Heading toward the main section of campus, I ran—past the lights and traffic on Central Road, past stragglers trudging home from the library and gym. My

lungs ached but I kept going, past the building where I'd
first seen Dhani, up the cement walkways, through a desolate
stretch of wind tunnel far off by the fine arts center. It was
quiet there. Nobody came to this place at night. I turned
back to look at my school, thinking about how bright it had
looked the first day of snow and how ugly it seemed now, all
buried. I thought of the way the blob had looked at the end
of the Steve McQueen movie, draped heavily across the diner
before they froze it. Then I felt my knees give.

Sometime later it occurred to me that I was actually lying
in the snow. But I could think of no reason to move and so
rolled slowly onto my side, imagining what a lumpy sick
snow angel I might make. I had a memory: running this way
once before, on my way home one night back in high school.
My stomach had hurt then too. I'd felt afraid—of Steve, of
Rainbo and Val for some reason, and of falling. But I guessed
that my earlier flight had taken place in a dream. If I had
really run from Steve, from those girls, if I had been strong
enough somehow to escape, surely I would not now be lying
in snow. I put my fist down into new powder and let it sink
in toward my body until, very gradually, I was slapping my
stomach. Several minutes later, numb as if shot through with
novocaine, I stood and walked home. Christina was out. My
silver graduation tray, dented as if someone had kicked it, was
on the floor by my bed.

I went to the Christmas dorm party wearing Gwyn's torn
sweater and the girdle, which pinched. People were polite.
We exchanged little gifts and kisses. After Laroo shoved her,
Christina hugged me. Walking back upstairs, I wondered if
they had met one night in Laroo's room to discuss me. It
occurred to me that they'd known all along. But I couldn't be
sure. No one, not one girl, not one professor had ever men-

tioned it. No one commented now on the fact that, as I prepared to leave for the holidays, I was wearing two pairs of jeans I had turned sloppily into a skirt beneath a long sweat-shirt cut up to the armpits. I was constantly gasping for breath, but when it came time to go, December 22, we said only, "Bye, now—have a great fuckin' break."

I took my red flowered suitcase and walked down the stairs sideways. "Merry Christmas," girls called out on the land-ings. "You too," I wheezed. Outside the snow seemed to have stopped, or perhaps it had stopped a few days earlier and I had not noticed. But it looked tougher out there now than before. The fluffy white drifts had hardened into tiny ice-bergs. I walked quickly to the bus with my head down, as I had as a nonchalant, as a girl who was there but not there.

SIX

Seated on the bus, I draped a coat across my body as I might have a sleeping bag. I pictured a bed. I imagined myself in it, beneath a quilt, and slid down further inside my coat toward the floor. Suddenly I felt a pain in my shoulder. I opened my eyes. A large girl in white overalls was poking me. "Can you move over?" she said. I nodded. It was best, I concluded, not to think about beds, about anything, but to watch the road as we drove. I looked out the window and saw our luggage piled on the sidewalk. We had not yet left.

Four hours and ten minutes later, arriving in Utica, New York, the driver announced a stop. Passengers stretched and filed out, but not the girl in white overalls. I sighed impatiently as I waited. I gently nudged her. I contemplated stabbing her with a pen. Finally I said, "Please move," pushed past her and ran, stopping only when I stood inside the restaurant. Cutting in front of four others, I slammed the bathroom door and tore off the double-jeans skirt, as if fleeing an alien plant form. I exhaled and lowered myself onto the toilet. Time seemed pleasantly to slow. I was tired. I could easily have fallen asleep. Then someone knocked. I chose to ignore it and began, in a trance, to rock the blob, pressing it between my thighs, squeezing it with the fury unleashed most often on a pus-filled pimple. There was another knock. The door opened one inch and a girl in a powder-blue ski jacket gasped, said, "God, I'm sorry," and stepped out. "Hey, let's go," someone else called, and tucking in the blob, I walked out and back to the bus, a powder-blue chorus of "Look at that" echoing behind me.

Hours later my father appeared outside the window. He wore his old gray fedora at an angle over one eye and kept his hands buried inside winter coat pockets. I thought about how many times in my life my father had waited for me, about how, unlike other fathers, he had always been on time. I started to cry. The girl in the overalls said, "Yeah, it's good to be away from that place, I can relate totally." I wiped my nose on my coat sleeve, nodded and found myself suddenly off the bus. My father was carrying my bag. Kissing my forehead, he said, "You are home now."

As we drove through light snow, I tried to appear cheerful, speaking loudly about how soon I would be called upon to declare a major: It was a serious commitment, I said; one had to choose wisely.

"You're absolutely right," my father agreed. "I understand quite well. It is serious, and you'll have to think long and hard. For now, is that seatbelt on too tight for you?"

"No, why?" I asked.

"Just asking," he said, and I waited in fear of what he'd ask next. But he just hummed along to the "Swingin'-est Swing" program on the AM. And I myself felt strangely calm, as if I were being zippered into a large dark garment bag, the top closing securely over my head the more lights on the parkway we passed.

At lunch the next day, I continued to speak about how difficult it would be to choose a major. As I spoke, people disappeared. Sashi hugged me and left for ballet class. My parents went to buy last-minute gifts at the mall. Gwyn and a friend who'd said, "Too many munchies up there, huh?" ran out behind them. I called a few of my friends. No one was home. I went out for a walk and kept walking until I'd reached Steve's.

Steve, it seemed, was asleep, "drunk as a skunk," said his mother. I waited in the basement, facing a wall. I studied the Pompeii-theme wallpaper, concentrating on the townsman who points to the volcano using a mutton chop. Someone had drawn a beard on his wife. I asked Steve's mother about it. "No," she said, nodding, "she's always had a beard." Looking at me, she added, "You've lost weight. Your face looks thin."

I sighed with relief. Steve came down, belched, and kissed me without comment. Things, I sensed, were in a holding pattern. I agreed to go with Steve to see his father.

Mr. Bono, whom I'd met just once before, had moved to Babylon, to a singles condo unit consisting of a tiny balcony and what he called the "snazz crushed-velvet living area." It looked to me like an empty room with some large pillows and floor-to-ceiling orange carpet. As we sat at the area's center sipping whiskey sours, Mr. Bono leaned over to pat the top of the blob.

"Looks like you've put on a little weight there, Beth," he said. I denied it. He said, "Yes, look," and Steve said, "No, she's fine, let's drop it." I went into the bathroom, where the orange carpet even ran along the ceiling. I sat there twenty minutes, waiting for Steve to bang on the door so that I could tell him I wanted to leave.

Driving home, Steve said, "Okay, so maybe you're not pregnant. But why don't you at least do exercises? Then you won't have to be upset by what people say."

It was suddenly cold in the car. A chalky taste coated my tongue. I remembered once at Caro's being very stoned and licking an ashtray on a dare. Soon, it seemed, I'd no longer have such unpredictable thoughts. I'd no longer be so nervous, I'd be simply exhausted, falling asleep in unlikely places, possibly dead. A pain stuck my side. "Steve," I said, "I just want to go home. I don't want to talk about this."

On Winter Festival eve, I stood in front of the mirror and tried to admire my outfit—the two-jeans skirt, a bulky sweater and then another sweater over that. It looked terrible. I practiced making conversation that, for a time, might keep others from noticing. "Hi," I said, "great to see you," which I varied with, "Hi. I earned a 3.55 cumulative grade point average." This sounded ridiculous. I walked downstairs.

After standing on the bottom step several minutes, I began to prepare the holiday sock tree, the candy-striped pole we used for stockings in the absence of a fireplace. I made piles on the floor before me: the tinfoil stars, Sashi's string-and-glue balls, the angels made of wooden spools. Blinking white window lights tossed sudden shadows onto the walls. The room smelled of wassail and cinnamon. For a moment I felt at peace. Then I felt my father's hand on my shoulder. He was sitting at my side, working his way around on the floor to face me. I tried to turn in the other direction but he held my arm, put a hand on the blob and said, "You'll have to lose this."

"Please, Daddy," I said, rolling up, "I am very tired of all these comments." I walked to the kitchen, where my sisters were icing the reindeer cakes. I walked upstairs to the bathroom and stared at myself in the mirror. I heard noises downstairs and one voice, Aunt Ruth's, calling, "Where is she? Where is the student?"

"I'm coming," I called as I ran back into my room. I put another sweater over the two. I looked like an Eskimo woman. Two seconds later Ruth was tugging on my cheek. "So," she said, squealing, "Report!"

I said, "It's really great. I have the best friends in the world up there," and held my breath, waiting for her eyes to drop, followed rapidly by her mouth. But Aunt Ruth was talking about Yale, about Gothic architecture, about how, in a photo my mother had shown her, my campus had lacked mature trees. "Donnie is headed for the law school—an early admission," she said. "Lisette will be spending the winter doing marble in Carrara—that's in Italy, sweetheart." Ruth talked on, oblivious. I felt something wet roll down my leg, said, "Excuse me please," and ran back upstairs to the bathroom.

Vaguely I expected to see blood, but found nothing. "I'm

hallucinating," I said to the mirror. This thought was frightening. At the same time it seemed the next logical step. It might also have helped clarify certain perceptions. I had sensed, for example, that my parents were watching me, tracking my every move with their eyes, trailing from room to room behind me. If I mentioned this, my father, as spokesman, would say, "Why would we be watching you? Can you tell me why we might be concerned?" The answer could well be: They weren't looking; I was the victim of paranoid fantasies.

Back in the playroom I kept my eyes on both parents, testing my theory. I moved to the reclining chair. I got out the tinsel, picked up my present from Aunt Ruth, and looked up each time to find us all eye to eye. There was no mistaking it: They *were* staring. I looked for Gwyn and saw her comparing nails with Donnie's girlfriend; I looked for Sashi, but she was in the corner, patiently smiling as Uncle Benny asked, "Do you want to leave out Santa's cookie?" I opened my present from Aunt Ruth. It was a sweater. I looked around again for people, besides my parents, I might talk to. I was turning in a circle. Coco, who thought I was playing, jumped at my heels. Kneeling down I said, "Let's go for a walk, okay?" but she pulled away, ran to fake-Cousin Lisette and jumped into her lap.

Christmas morning, I opened my gifts, put on my many sweaters and walked the several miles to Steve's. As I arrived, his little brothers were destroying their new space toys because they'd looked smaller unwrapped in the living room than they had on TV. I sat down, exhausted, to examine the wreckage. Steve sat down next to me, opened a beer and put his hand on my knee. Leaning over, he whispered, "I'm horny." I looked at the ceiling, so drained of energy I could not imagine acting out the next five minutes of my life. "Don't worry," he whispered, "I'll use a rubber." I was much too tired to argue this nor anything and let him lead me by a wrist up to his room.

We had not had sex since my trip to Steve's school in October. At Thanksgiving I had pleaded bad cramps; the night of the big party I'd claimed nerves due to finals. Undressing on December 25, I realized that I had run out of excuses. Steve sat up in bed. "Look at that," he said. "Are you sure you're not pregnant?" I said that I was sure and that if he didn't stop scaring me I would go back to my house, where I belonged. Placing my hand around his penis, Steve said that he would never scare me. "You can just leave your shirt on," he added.

Sometime later he rolled off me as if from a sand dune. He said, "You really should lose weight."

I thought about this, attempting as I had that last time with Dhani to say the first thing that came into mind. "Steve," I finally said, "I think for now I need some coffee."

Steve agreed and drove me to the Shore East Diner. The place was crowded. People clotted the aisle by the cash register; others stared down into the lobster tank, their faces violet with fluorescent glow. I stayed off to one side near the coat check as Steve parked the car. But even there I noticed someone staring — a girl with heavy purple liner and a red leather jumpsuit. As she moved her eyes up my body I recognized Hilaree Crane, fully grown but still vaguely oriental. She introduced two guys from London.

"So," I said, turning away toward the coats, "I'm about to graduate college early. I'm becoming an actress. I already have parts." I had no idea why I was saying this. "How about you?" I asked, hoping to say nothing more.

Hilaree laughed and said, "Well, it's a long way — wherever — from hanging around inside the Shore East bathroom."

One of the British guys asked, "So what did you ladies do hanging around in a bathroom?"

"Oh, you know," Hilaree said, rolling her eyes, "killin' time with totally dumb ideas about sex, gossip, cigarettes, whaddya do in case . . . well, you know, the usual."

Thinking about the bathroom, I felt flushed. I stopped smiling. One British guy winked and said, "Good luck with your acting." Hilaree spit out a giggle. "Yeah," she said. "Good to see ya, Merry Christmas." Looking once more at my stomach, she walked out. Steve, on his way in from the parking lot, snapped his fingers. "What's going on now?" he said.

"I forgot that it was Christmas," I told him. "I have to go home."

In bed a few minutes later, I considered what would happen if I poured something—alcohol or iodine—inside of me to end this situation. I tried to picture what my mother would do when she found either me or the blood on the sheets. I dropped this idea and thought about my friends. It was early, only 9:00, and it seemed that I should get up to make phone calls. But nobody would be home. Caro would be out, driving around with the younger girls or with Rainbo; Val had disappeared from my life as I'd once overnight departed hers. I told myself that I wished her well, then sat straight up in bed. "I don't care about Victor," I said out loud, "she should call me. I really have to talk to someone."

But I knew that if I got up to call Val or Caro, to find Gwyn, who had boyfriends now and went out, that I'd run into my parents and have to flee. They were constantly asking me how I was, following me around the house, transmitting whispered messages over my shoulder. I thought instead about having a cigarette. I pictured dropping it, then falling, dizzy, down the stairs. It might not be so bad. Then they could look at me lying there. Something would be said about why and this would end.

On December 31, I decided the only way to face my fears was to go out of the house to find my friends. I told Steve, whom I'd avoided since Christmas, that I wanted to party. Steve said, "Okay, if you really want to." If I was sure, he said, we could go later on to Johnny Mac's, a popular bar by the Massapequa train station. I said, "Great, let's go." Steve inhaled and said, "If you really want."

There were the standard kids outside Johnny Mac's that night: the girls with eyes oozy as Vaseline; the guys toking so hard off hash pipes their cheeks turned purple. Inside there were about a hundred others, all talking at once, shouting, passing things. It was so loud and confusing I ignored Steve's saying, "Okay, take off your coat." I just stood there. "Well," he said, "at least get away from the door." When I failed to respond, he pulled me into a corner. "Wait here," he said sternly, "I'll get us a table."

I looked at the secretarial girls, Debbie and Karen and the others, all standing at the bar, each with one foot balanced on the rung of a stool. They seemed to have been choreographed, like the June Taylor Dancers—lifting cigarettes to mouths in perfect succession, leaning for ashtrays in sequence. I wondered if they were aware of it, but Steve reappeared and pulled me by a sleeve through the crowd. "Okay," he said as we reached a small round table the size of a Frisbee, "sit here."

People approached and asked me questions about school. I'd start to answer them but they'd see someone else, say, "Check ya out later," and move on. Caro came by. She kissed me and said, "I have your present," then ran outside with

Rainbo Martin, who would not say hello at all because, according to Caro, "You didn't go out with the girls once this vacation. You think you are superior." I looked over at the secretarial girls—all of them staring at me, opening and closing their mouths rhythmically as fish. I said, "I *am* superior." Jason, who'd dropped down into the chair next to me, said, "You're what?"

I tried to picture having sex with Jason, something I had pictured a million times since age twelve, but could not. Jason chatted a few minutes with someone else, then, tipping an inch-long ash from his cigarette, said, "Bets. Looks as if you've put on weight since I saw you. What's going on?" I started reciting facts about Calverton, but a hand had landed on my shoulder. I looked up to see Boat Brody, who lowered his other hand and touched the blob.

"What's that?" he shouted above the noise. "Is it a baby? Are you gonna have a kid or what?"

I jumped up, almost spilling the table. "No," I whispered, backing away, "it's nothing, no."

"Calm down," Jason said, winking at Boat. He leaned up to hug a thin girl wearing a black leotard, faded jeans and pink hoop earrings. The girl hugged Boat and all three— Boat, the girl and Jason—stared at me as I backed up into the crowd. I was thick inside it one second later, crushed up against tall girls in jeans that had labels, turning and ending up with my face in the backs of sweatshirts, near gold chokers, in cigarettes. "Help me," I called, "I have to get out." In response another hand landed on the back of my neck. "I'm really sorry," Boat said, his voice as low and sexy as a moan. "Ya know, I didn't mean to embarrass you. I'm sure you just gained weight." I thought back to seeing Hilaree in the diner and of the way Caro had run out of the bar. Boat mumbled something else and I thought further back, to the way his voice had sounded—to the way those two girls had sat there smiling—at Steve's New Year's Eve party years before. People began to count backward from sixty, shouting the numbers, raising fists and beer bottles into the air. I started to scream. One girl pushed me and said, "Chill out." Another said, "Shut the fuck up." When I finally turned, I saw not Boat but Steve, working his way through the crowd to where I crouched.

He pulled me out to the sidewalk. Behind us people shrieked, "Fuckin' 1977." In front of us, Big Chief Lewis and his faithful bison cub looked shiny and wet, star-burst as tears collected at the edges of my eyes.

After New Year's I stayed in the house. I listened to the radio. I tried to think of people to call besides Steve and thought of Darren Shapiro, the artist boys had always made fun of. Val had written once just to say that he was gay, which suggested that perhaps he'd be sympathetic. I called him one afternoon. He was not home. After hanging up the phone, I walked back to my room and just stayed there.

On January 12, four days before I was scheduled to return to college, my father knocked on my door and said that he and my mother wanted to talk to me. I worked my way out of the beanbag chair and followed him down to the kitchen. Seated at my place, I thought the chair seemed kind of far from the placemat, as if the table had been moved. It was quiet in the room. Dust particles tangled in the sunlight. My father leaned back in his chair and turned to face me.

"Your mother and I are both extremely proud of how well you have adjusted to your new life," he said. "And we are especially proud that you made the dean's list."

I smiled. I had forgotten about the dean's list. "Very

proud," he said. "We think it's quite wonderful. And," he added, leaning forward, "we also think—no, we know—that you are pregnant."

I said what I had said to Steve, to my mother, to myself: "I am not," and felt a cramp pinch my side.

My father folded his hands. "Okay," he said, "so you tell us, what is this strange way you have gained weight?"

"I don't know," I said, my voice sounding thin, airy as a whistle blown too lightly. "I don't know," I said again. I tried to stand. My father clamped a hand on top of mine. "I think you do know," he said. "You've known, as we've known, for some time. Now, your mother and I had hoped that you would admit what has happened on your own. But we've waited long enough. There is a serious problem here, and we are going to have to deal with it. Let's get you over to Goldberg, your mother's doctor. He'll tell us in three minutes what's up."

"No."

My mother said, "Well, sweetheart, maybe it's something other than what it seems to be, okay? But whatever it is, we have to find out now. Enough time has passed, okay?"

"Please talk to us," my father said.

My mother asked, "Think, Betsy, did you use all those tampons you bought, did you use any of them? . . ."

"Leave me alone," I shouted, getting up from the table, "just leave me goddamned alone," and I ran down to the playroom, into the little bathroom I'd avoided ever since the day, in fifth grade, I'd found a spider floating in the toilet. I closed the door and stood there. I turned to face a wall. I picked up a magazine, dropped it and turned to look in the mirror. I turned again and started to pull Dixie cups, one at a time, from the dispenser. I tossed them over my shoulder. My father was standing behind me and caught one.

"Let's go into my office," he said, holding out his hand. "C'mon."

My mother was waiting there with her mouth pinched. My father lowered me into a chair by his desk and spoke slowly. "You are obviously pregnant," he said. "And I am afraid that it may be too late to abort. But we'll bring you over this afternoon to find out for certain." He put his arm around me and I started to cry. My mother was dialing the phone. "Yes," she said to the person at the other end, "it looks serious." I buried my face in my father's sweater and felt the tension or fear or whatever I had tried to hold in explode.

S E V E N

Dr. Goldberg's office was hot as a sauna. Twenty women sat on the couches, magazines to their chests instead of towels.

"Are you sure there's only one doctor here?" I asked my mother.

"Welcome to the wonderful world of gynecologists," she whispered, "why don't you take off your coat?"

I kept it on, sat down and watched a girl my age in a black lacy top. She looked like a secretarial girl: uncombed dirty-blond hair, freckles like dots, gum snapped so vigorously you could see blackish fillings at the back of her mouth. She was obviously pregnant, as I now was obviously pregnant. But this girl—reading *People* magazine, humming along to "Come Saturday Morning"—looked like someone who might reasonably be pregnant. I wanted somehow to convey that I had nothing in common with her, but she waddled off to the bathroom before I had a chance. An hour passed. The girl removed her gum, stuck it on her magazine and disappeared with a white-shoed nurse around a corner. Half an hour after that a nurse with a modified blond beehive looked right at me. "Okay, honey," she said, "let's go."

Inside the examining room she pointed to a steel table and said, "Everything off. Up there." Forty-five minutes later I heard masculine chuckling outside the door, and fifteen minutes after that Dr. Sy Goldberg, the man who had delivered both my sisters—along with 80 percent of young southern Long Island—stepped in holding a folder. From the door he glanced at me and whistled.

"Baby," he said, rolling me down, "why the hell'd you wait so long? We've got a belly here."

"I want an abortion," I said, as I'd said earlier to my father. I sat back up.

Easing me down, he said, "Honey, that's a belly. Now stay put."

"I want an abortion," I shouted, my nose colliding with my stomach.

Dr. Goldberg spoke from the counter, where he was assembling a tool that looked like a flashlight. "Baby, we'll do salines up to twenty weeks, but you're beyond that by a month, maybe more. Now listen." He placed the instrument, some kind of stethoscope, against the blob. What I heard was a slurping, purring noise, the sound of a pool filter at night. Taking my hand, he said, "Sweetheart. That's a heartbeat. There's nothing we can do about this now."

"I want an abortion," I whimpered. But Dr. Goldberg was halfway out the door. "Get dressed quickly," he called from the hallway. "I will meet with you and your mother in my office."

The doctor spoke to my mother without looking at me. He explained that he had seen "things" like this before, although "usually not so far gone." He reviewed the reasons why he could not perform a saline, then said that he would give her the name of an attorney he called "the best." Using all my strength, I lifted my head. "What about school?" I asked.

Dr. Goldberg looked at me as if I were a secretary who had dared speak during a policy meeting. "Sweetheart," he said, chuckling, "you want to go back with that belly? You'll be the laughingstock of the entire campus. Now, maybe there are homes in the area you could investigate. You discuss it with Mom and Dad." Lowering his voice, he talked again to my mother.

"What about school?" I said. The beehive nurse came in with some water. "What about school?" I asked her. My mother dropped one hand on my knee and reached with the other to take the paper Dr. Goldberg had written on. "Give Larry Stein a call," he said, "Stein is your man." The nurse was trying to move me. Dr. Goldberg was coming around the desk, tucking a pen into his white lab-coat pocket. He placed one hand on my mother's shoulder. I shouted, "I want to know about school." All three of them looked at me. The doctor took a step forward and reached for my hand. He said, "I'm sorry." I turned and ran back through the waiting room. The girl in the black lacy top was standing by the closet and jumped out of my way. My mother was behind me. "Honey, um, take it easy," she called tentatively, as if by surprise she'd found herself with a pregnant person.

In the car I mouthed the one word I could think of relating to my situation. It happened to be *suicide*. When I began saying it out loud, my mother pulled over. "Now, you listen," she said angrily, "you will get through this somehow, none of this suicide stuff." She said this again. I drooped against the door. "Betsy," my mother said, and I shouted, "I can't have a baby. I don't want it. My life will be ruined forever. It's not fucking fair, it's not fair." I sat up, considering this, then leaned over to grab my mother's sleeve. "No," I shrieked as she pulled out, "no way."

My mother drove quickly through slushy streets. At home my father held open the screen door, saying, "So?"

"I can't believe this," I mumbled, walking past him to the stairs. I heard my mother say, "Seven, give or take," and then the sound of their steps coming to get me.

It was dark in the kitchen. Something sticky on the placemat caught my bathrobe sleeve. My father spoke. "We have much to do here," he began. "You will have many important decisions to make in the near future, so let me say first that we are not in any way angry at you, nor are we disappointed. This is just something that has unfortunately happened in your life and you—we—will deal with it. Someday you will see that it forms just a piece, a chapter, of your history. Which isn't to say that it will be easy for you, just that you will survive it."

"Now," he continued, unscrewing the top of his fountain pen, "I am going to make a list of my concerns, and you and your mother will list yours independently. Then we'll go through them one at a time."

I stood up. "I am not going to have this," I announced. "It's not fair. I'm going back to school."

My mother, who'd sat with her hands folded, looked at me and sighed. My father glanced up from where he'd written *leave of absence/adoption if it comes to it?* and said, "You will have this child because, quite simply, you have no choice." Enunciating carefully, he added, "And you will do the honorable thing. You will accept this child as yours, as *ours*. If we must, your mother and I will raise it ourselves."

"It's not your fucking choice," I shouted, trying to pass in back of his chair. "It's not yours at all and I won't fucking have this and you can't make me. So just fucking forget it." I ran upstairs.

My father went on to shout about honor and adolescent irresponsibility; my mother said, "Honey, please. We have to attack this rationally." I felt, lying face down in the beanbag, as if I'd woken up inside a Health class movie.

"Okay," my mother said, coming in a while later, "just between us for now. Let's take things one step at a time. The first order of business, I'm afraid, is that you'll have to call Steve. He has to know what's going on."

I considered saying that, for her information, the father was a boy whom I loved—Dhani or Jason—and not Steve. But I decided against it. Rolling over, I said, "I'll call him. But I will not have this. I'm having an abortion and you can tell your fucking husband to mind his own goddamned business."

"For God's sake, Betsy," my mother said as I walked to the phone in her room. "Please don't make this any more difficult than it already is."

Steve picked up and asked, "Where were you just now?"

I replied, my voice shaking, "At the doctor's."

"I knew it," he shouted. "I'm sittin' in my room saying 'if she ain't home then she's there.' Fuck. Well what the fuck did he say?"

I was crying. "He said I have to have it. I don't want it. I don't want you. I have to get out of here."

"Hold on, babe," Steve said, his voice suddenly deep, "don't panic, just—"

"My mother says you have to come over and don't you fucking dare tell anyone, Steven Bono, do you understand me? Or I will kill you, do you understand?"

"I'll do whatever you want."

"You better or—I'm serious, Steve—you will be dead. There will be a bullet in you. So you better be here at six."

My father was standing in the door frame as I hung up, his right eye twitching. "Is that bastard going to get his ass over here?"

"Yes, six o'clock, Herr Hitler, as requested."

"Don't you give me that crap, young lady," he shouted, following me down the hall to my room. "I will not take that crap from you or from anyone, do you understand me?" I tried to close my bedroom door in his face but he pushed it in. I said, "I'm going back to school." He said, "You will stay here and finish your term because you have no choice." My mother, appearing suddenly, said, "Both of you—enough."

At six o'clock the doorbell rang. Steve grunted at me and said hello to my sisters, who said "Hi" from the table without looking up. Steve was a mess. His eyes were so red they looked veiny; his arms dangled, monkeylike, from the sleeves of an old pea coat. "Well, let's go," my mother said without greeting him, and we walked downstairs just as my father walked out from his workroom. Clearing his throat, sitting down in the recliner, my father said, "All right. Let's get on with it." He paused, then, like Hercule Poirot addressing the suspects at mystery's end, proclaimed, "This is the situation."

I was, he said slowly, seven months and an unknown

number of days pregnant—in any event, too far along for an abortion, which would have been the desired solution. My inclination, he continued, seemed to be to place the child with an adoptive family, although this was not the resolution he favored. Steven, it was assumed, would lend full cooperation. My father looked at him for the first time. Steve was watching Coco roll over onto her back.

"Is that clear?" my father said, but Steve just sat there. "Mr. Bono, do I have your attention?"

"Yeah," Steve said at last.

"Well, then, since I have such an excellent audience, let me make one other thing clear. It's this, sir. You have—though I am to blame for having tolerated your presence this long against better judgment—dishonored my daughter and this family. I never so long as I shall live want to see your mutt face in this house again, or I will have your freaking ass served up on a police platter. Do I make myself clear, sir?"

Steve said, "Yup."

"Fine, then," he continued. "A Mr. Lawrence Stein, an attorney specializing in adoption proceedings, will contact you shortly. I expect that out of respect for my daughter and in consideration of the damage you have caused, you will cooperate with him fully. You may take your leave of us, effective immediately."

My father walked out. My mother walked Steve to the door, and I walked to my room and kicked the beanbag. Half an hour later my mother knocked and entered at the same time. She looked around. "Sweetheart," she asked, folding her arms, "what are you doing with your suitcase?"

"I'm packing," I told her, wiping my nose on a bra. "I'm not staying here. I'm going back."

My mother sighed. "Sweetie, you cannot leave this house. You may do whatever you like as soon as this is over, okay?"

"Get out," I shouted, "get the fuck out." My mother rolled her eyes and closed the door. I turned and found myself facing the mirror. My body was swollen and pale, mimicking the general contour and color of an egg. My hair hung in damp strips just past my shoulders. It was the bloated, blank look that I had in the past associated with people who'd drowned.

The next morning, my mother came in to tell me what they had done.

First they had told my sisters. Gwyn had said, "I knew it." Sashi had cried and asked if, technically, the baby would be our relative, and if so in whose room it would sleep. Then my father had called Calverton to arrange for a leave of absence. "He told them you had mono, honey," my mother said, rubbing my knee. "Now, I think you'll need to talk to your sisters and to back the mono story by telling Christina yourself." It was hard to say which speech would be worse. I sat there for a few minutes, put on my robe and called Christina.

My roommate paused when I told her, thought a minute and said, "That's too bad, roomie, about the mono. So, make sure you send what you owe on the phone, okay? You made all these long-distance calls, like thirty seconds each, the last week." I tried to remember what calls these were. I tried to think of something else to say to Christina, but my roommate yawned, said, "Take care," and hung up. I walked as if in a trance down to meet with my sisters. Sitting cross-legged on the playroom floor, I said, "This is a terrible tragedy, but it is not one that you, as members of the younger generation, need suffer." I stopped and started crying. Sashi, trying to keep her eyes off my stomach, said, "If you want us to do anything just say it and we will." Touching my shoulder, Gwyn added, "I'll take care of gossip and the nosy outside world."

"Speaking of which," my mother said on her way into the room, "you'll need a friend."

"Caro?" my father said, following behind her, "although you've known Val longer."

I thought of the way Caro had run out with Rainbo at Johnny Mac's and never called me. Val I'd barely spoken to since graduation. "No," I said. "They can't be trusted. I don't want them or anyone—not even our grandparents—to know. It's none of anyone's business. I just want to stay in my room."

"Very well," my father said, looking down at his yellow pad. "Let us review what we've accomplished. The lawyer will be here tomorrow, but we must think first and not make knee-jerk decisions about things that will affect us the rest of our lives. This child *is* ours. Regardless of exact parentage, it has the right to a decent upbringing within this family, and I intend to see that he or she gets it."

I began to pull on my hair. My mother led Gwyn and Sashi up to the kitchen. "It is not," I said slowly, "for the fortieth time, your goddamned decision to make. I do not want this kid. That is it. I fucking hate it. I hate it! I hate you!"

"Your feelings for me are irrelevant," he said, starting to shout. "You, Elizabeth Ann Israel, placed yourself into this situation, and now, as an adult, you will do—so help me, God—the responsible thing. And you will watch your language."

"That's enough," my mother said, walking back down the stairs. Coming to a stop, she looked at me, then at my father. "Honey," she said quietly, "her decision has been made. And it is *her* decision to make, not yours. That, I'm afraid, is that."

• • •

My mother, because I'd asked, had arranged for me to have one last date with Steve, and at eight that night I walked down the block to his car, dressed in jeans the size of a small camping tent held up with suspenders. I had found this outfit on my bed, wondered who it possibly could have been for and then remembered. Steve opened the car door and said, "What the fuck are you wearing?"

"Steve," I said, "just drive—anywhere." He drove around the block to the Nautilus Diner and parked in the lot. Sitting there staring at my suspenders, Steve told me what his parents had said. His mother had mumbled, "God help us all," then had drunk a tall glass of vodka straight without breathing. His father had punched him in the side of the head and said, "Nice work, asshole." I started to cry. Steve took my hand. When it was over, he said, we would go out to dinner on the North Shore. We would go jogging. He would get me clothes. I stared off into the back swamps of Zappaland and cried harder.

Steve said, "Marry me, babe."

Sniffling, I said, "Give me a fucking break."

Steve punched the steering wheel. "Why the fuck not?" he shouted, "You don't love me that way? You think you're so superior?"

"Steve," I said, "even if I did love you that way—which I don't—I wouldn't marry you. It would ruin my entire life."

"Well, then let me fuckin' see it," he demanded.

"See what?" I asked. "What do you want to see?"

Steve stared into the dark heart of Zappa. "I want to see what I did to you. I want to see it."

"It's pretty gross, Steve," I cautioned, unhooking the suspenders.

In the filmy light of the Nautilus Diner sign the blob rose up out of my jeans, a glowing white orb crossed with red tracks and now a thin brown line. I studied this new line. Steve's head fell onto the steering wheel with a thud as if he'd been shot.

"I warned you," I said, but Steve was backing out across Merrick Road toward the canal. I tried to change the subject. "Steve," I said, scanning the water, "where's the old barge? Did someone finally come to take it? It's gone."

Steve turned on two wheels up Moccasin. He said, "It sunk."

On January 16, the day I was supposed to return to school, Larry Stein, a Manhattan lawyer wearing a toupee and a tight pin-striped vest, came for tea. He took off his shoes, sat on the couch in half-lotus position and spoke energetically to my parents. He discussed "selection" and "payment"; he reviewed a legal matter called "the right-to-discovery clause" the way a kid might describe his camp activities. My parents, nodding, asking the occasional question, looked surprisingly old: Their skin seemed to be loose on the bone; their hair was gray, as if the dust circling the kitchen the day we'd talked had stuck. When they looked at me, when the lawyer said, "You seem like one great, one truly super kid," I would smile. For most of the conversation I just sat there listening to the snow blow off the roof, picturing with my eyes closed the local roads that led to the highways and then the parkways out of town.

After the lawyer had gone I went up to my room and tried, for the first time, to consider the baby as a person.

I began by reviewing the fact that there actually *was* a baby. Out loud I said, "The blob is not skin. It is a baby." Elaborating, I recited, "I am responsible for this poor, innocent, helpless little creature." Next I tried picturing a baby's face. What I pictured, however, was not a baby's face but Steve's, which I followed as it got into a car and drove off back to junior college. It was possible there would be other people in the car. It was possible that Steve would break down and tell. It seemed critical that people not think I'd dropped out! I constructed mental lists of things to do so that people, my sisters included, would know this. I made a second list of all I'd do, by day and week, as soon as I was free. I looked up, trying to remember what I had set out to picture. Looking down, I noticed my bathrobe parted and a new stretch mark etched on my thigh. My mother came in. I started crying.

It seemed that Steve was on the phone. He'd called to say that he'd be going back to school in the morning and that he'd be going out to a party that night. "I gotta tell people again that you're sick," he explained, "they're all gossiping like crazy." Steve filled in the details, but I calmly replaced the receiver so that I would not have to hear them.

Back in my room I found a red spiral notebook on the desk. A fancy black fountain pen lay across the cover. My father had used it to write, on page one, *Just one of life's unexpected chapters*.

My routine, mid-January, consisted of this: Waking late, I would try to remember what I was doing at home in my room. Quickly remembering, I would pronounce the word "fuck," then walk as slowly as I could into the bathroom. I'd run the shower. I liked the sound of the water, it was soothing, even though I would no longer remove my clothes to get in. The day Steve left, I'd seen what looked like a tiny fist poke the top of the blob and had vowed from then on to stay dressed. I'd sit for a while listening to the water, then, wearing suspender pants and bathrobe, I'd walk downstairs. I might, after breakfast, make a cake from a mix or work at an invented chore of my mother's. When that grew dull I resumed eating—cookies, bagels, toast, cheese—read old novels off my parents' shelves and waited for calls or the mailman.

On January 21 my mother slipped a letter from Dhani beneath my door. He had won his battle with Erie Dining Hall: Now they would serve bulgur! I was ecstatic, although I had never heard of bulgur. On January 22 there was a letter from Christina. It said, *It's still snowing here, as you can guess. Right now you still owe $17.82 on the phone. Please write the check now or I will have to call your mother.* On the twenty-third there was something from Steve. He had traced pictures of Goofy and Porky Pig onto index cards. *Keep up your smile,* he'd scribbled along the bottom. Caro called the same evening. I was asleep.

There was no mail after that, and the only person who called—every day—was Mr. Stein. Souped up as a DJ, he'd say, "The main thing, babe, is that you get plenty of rest, take vitamins, tell me *anything* that's on your mind and be sure to think about the discovery clause—the contract point that says you keep those files open, okay, babe? Gotta have your okay—either way." My mother drove me Thursdays to see the doctor, who looked at me pityingly as if I had cancer and said, "You're eating too much." Back at home one late January day I wrote: *It's a relief (slight) not to lie anymore. That poor, sad girl. The important thing is that I'll pass through this, into the hospital and back out into "later," whatever later is. I guess you're not "my best friend," but I will tell how it goes—and how I am surviving, which I will (survive), or I will kill myself.*

By the end of January my family had settled uncomfortably into a routine of its own.

My father seemed to be around more than anyone. The steel construction company he'd run with fake-Uncle Benny had folded. One of his oldest friends from high school had died and he was depressed, my mother said; he needed time to think things through. No matter where I went that month I found him thinking—writing on a pad at the kitchen table; lying on the living room couch, a World War II sea novel draped across his chest.

How was I really? he'd ask as I passed. Was I practicing my flute, studying French? Did I want to speak in French on a regular basis, say ten minutes per day? I did not want to talk to my father in French or in English. I did not wish to speak to anyone, a position I'd explain as I walked off. My father, following me, would state his: "My situation is deplorable," he'd shout. "Yours, child, is finite, so come to terms and don't let your mind rot!" I'd jog up the stairs. Gwyn would turn the volume up on her stereo. Sashi would park herself outside my door as I slammed it.

My sisters both were cautious, treating me as they might have a grandparent who'd come unexpectedly to stay. The first day of February I opened my door and almost stepped on Sashi, who tumbled onto the rug. Sitting up, she asked, "So, do you think I could please sometime touch your stomach?" Hoping to seem casual, adult, I shrugged and said, "Touch it now." Sashi reached out a hand and gasped, "It's hard." I threw her out, heard Gwyn on her way up the stairs and wedged a chair beneath the doorknob.

Gwyn had lost weight. She blow-dried her hair. She went out disco dancing in tight-fitting jeans she'd inspect in my full-length mirror the second I left for the bathroom. I could not bear to picture her waist or her going out, or the guy named Rick who stood in the living room saying, "Yeah, far out" to whatever my mother said. "Please," I'd scream when she knocked, "I'm busy."

Hours could pass as I sat guarding my door. At last I'd hear the grinding sound of plates pulled down from the cabinet, five at once. I'd hear my mother in the kitchen soothing my father, telling Gwyn to hold still as she fixed a hem, explaining to Sashi why I didn't care to join them as she placed one plate for me on a tray.

By mid-February I had ceased to get dressed. The blob seemed to me beyond clothes—streaked with purplish squiggles, the skin around it flabby like the fatty hem on a steak. I hid it much of the time beneath blankets. Sashi, by silent agreement, helped: I polished her tiny nails and let her try on makeup; she changed the channels on the TV now in my room and snuck me in food. I came out to speak with Mr. Stein about what I called his "dancing discovery clause." Once, on Valentine's Day, I talked to Caro.

She sounded breathy and small, the way girls sounded when they sensed that they had gone too far and made you mad. "Are you sure you're okay?" she asked, and I said that I was not, that I was sick, which made her sigh. "Look," she told me, "I'm really sorry I was so busy at Christmas. I guess I felt like, you know, like you had gone away and changed and everything—I mean, like you looked down on us. But I'm really sorry you got sick. I'll come and visit you."

I said, "I'm contagious," and hung up.

Back under the covers, I ate a slice of the pound cake I'd made that morning, fantasizing about what Caro and I would do and eat when I was better. I imagined clothes she'd ask to borrow. I remembered that for now I was supposed to be angry and tried instead to think of Jason. Quickly dropping that, I resolved to picture the baby, concentrating so hard my cheeks turned red. Sashi looked up and said, "What's the matter?" I exhaled and lay back. I had tried countless times to picture this. But it was, each attempt, like masturbating and getting bored in the middle: I'd have to admit it wasn't going to happen.

"Nothing," I told her, brushing crumbs off the sheet. "Just get me some ice cream. Put Bosco on it, okay?"

By early March my parents had come to sound like Mr. Stein: They could talk only about the "discovery clause"—a contract provision guaranteeing the child the right to information someday about its natural parents. The lawyer, I figured, was eager to have the issue resolved so that negotiations could move speedily forward. My father was strictly emotional. He seemed to have accepted my decision, but forfeiting the right to any contact, ever, was to him still unthinkable. I tried again to consider his views, but as I wrote on March 5, *the idea of opening a door, some year in my real life, to find this stranger who has the nasty dimples of Steve, is so horrifying I must lie down.* The truth was, I wanted this stranger dead. Since you could not legally kill a baby, I told my mother one day at breakfast, I should at least be allowed to pretend this kid was dead: It seemed as much punishment to make me live, terrified he or she might show up as it was to suggest that I raise it.

"You should think about what your father is saying," she told me. "He's afraid for you. He thinks that someday you may want to know. You shouldn't burn bridges."

I wasn't burning them, I told her, I was blowing them up, and I stomped out of the room, resolved not to speak to my father, then cried for behaving like a bitch. To make things worse, it was getting warmer outside.

The second week of March, I stood on a chair by my window just to inhale. I heard the sounds of kids out on South Merrick Road, and then, somewhat louder, the sound of a breeze lifting the ruffly white curtains my mother had hung in September. It occurred to me that I might have suffered brain damage. Tiny sounds—water off a drainpipe, the wind

—seemed magnified, while the larger background noise of voices and cars was soft. As I was standing there considering this, Steve called from school.

"People are really talkin'," he said, but I was distracted, listening to my parents' door creak and to the kids still making their way down the street behind our house. I reminded myself that I would come out of this situation, passing through the hospital and into "later," as I had written. But sitting there, arms around a belly now the size of a beach ball, I could not really see how I'd ever get back together or become friends with other kids. "Rainbo was up here with Karen and Debbie, those girls you call 'the secretaries'," Steve said suddenly. "You shoulda heard what they were sayin' about you." The girls outside passed, on their way home from Tremor. Steve said, "The new rumor is that you got knocked up by some hippie Jew at school." But what I heard above Steve and the girls was the thud of an old clock on the living-room wall, its pendulum seeming to slow the longer I sat there.

On March 12, Mr. Stein called my mother to say that he had "narrowed the field" to three couples. He came by the house that afternoon, said, "You look great," and pulled from his briefcase the dittos describing each one. "They're all great, really super individuals," he told me. I nodded and read, hoping to find hidden clues revealing which one was best. But halfway through the second ditto—Mr. Stein chanting "great, loving people" like a mantra—I stopped reading. I kept picturing the "Dating Game" host, who'd described even the guys with wide mod ties as "hip and with it." Like the girl contestant, I could not, according to rules, view the choices. And there were not, in the end, a lot of clues to be found hidden in a ditto. When Mr. Stein said "superlative people!" I said, "Okay, Christ," and pointed—to a Jewish lawyer and his kindergarten-teacher wife from Connecticut. I said, "They seem fine."

Mr. Stein told me that I'd made an excellent decision. He said that he'd meet with Steven later that week for his consent, although my choice, of course, was basically final. I nodded and walked upstairs saying what I thought I should, under the circumstances, say. "It is a tragedy," I mumbled, "to be denied the right to witness your child's early years, or later ones." But my mind floated this time to Steve and to the ways he might make trouble.

Steve came home three days later to meet with the lawyer. When he called me he sounded annoyed. He said, "I see you picked Jews."

"So what?" I said. "What are you saying?"

"I'm not sayin' anything, I'm just sayin' you picked Jews."

"Fuck you, Steve. Please. Go fuck yourself, finally."

"Hey, you better watch it," he said slowly. "People are talking about you. Karen and Debbie saw you in the car with your mother the other day. They said you didn't look too sick. So what are people supposed to think? Rainbo goes around saying you don't have freakin' mono. I do what I can, but I can't control what people say."

"Steve," I practically spit, "you promised. It's bad enough. Don't you dare scare me."

"I'm tryin', babe, but it's not easy. Try havin' a little sympathy for *me*. I'm doing everything I can. So look, you wanna go out while I'm here?"

Steve had read about a Beatles film festival at the Johnny All-Weather Drive-In out on Sunrise. My mother cleared the date with my father, and at eight that night I snuck out the back gate and stepped into Steve's car. Steve watched me struggle with the seatbelt, muttered, "Christ," and pulled out, heading for the Amityville Jack-in-the-Box, where we'd get shakes.

As we pulled in Steve said, "Do you want to talk into the clown?"

"I can't reach the clown," I said.

"Great," Steve shouted, slapping the wheel. "You can't reach the fucking clown. This is what it comes down to: *You can't reach the fucking clown.*" He put the car in reverse, shouted, "Go fuck yourself" at the voice asking "Chocolate or strawberry?" and backed out.

Let It Be was on at the Johnny All-Weather, Paul's bearded face sandy and a little scratched across the old screen. Steve tried to attach the speaker to our car but could not make it stay. After fumbling with it a few minutes, he opened his door and started pulling out the wires.

"Should we move?" I asked.

Steve was kicking the pole. I leaned over to hit the horn. When the people around us began to do the same, Steve got back in. He stared straight ahead.

"Should we move, Steve?" I asked.

Steve turned to face me. "I'm fucking horny," he shouted. "You think things are only so hard for you, that you're the only one who has to suffer? Well, I haven't fuckin' got laid in months! I'm a nervous wreck. I can't concentrate in school."

"So what do you want me to do about it?"

"You have to help me out, babe."

"Steve, you must be kidding."

"Fine," he spit. "Sit there. See if I give a shit. I'll just have to help myself. Fine."

Steve climbed over the seat and sat behind me. I looked around, praying for escape as I had on the nights, years before, when Steve had stopped to piss on someone's lawn. A few minutes later I heard him grunt and then, as my eyes closed, felt the semen drip off my collar and onto my neck.

On March 15, Dr. Goldberg said it would be another three weeks, possibly more. Having sat in the house for two months refusing showers, I could not contemplate three minutes more. Walking ahead of my mother through the waiting room, I slammed into the girl with the lacy top, though she seemed drugged and didn't notice. I refused from that day on to leave my room.

I lay in the beanbag chair listening to ice melt off the roof, trying to guess whether it dripped onto pavement or leaves. I reread *Pride and Prejudice* because nothing could have seemed more irrelevant to my present life. On March 20 I wondered what it would be like to walk normally again but couldn't picture it. On March 21 I wondered about sex. If I applied to the blob the achievement-test skill of attempting to figure out, from the pieces, what a box would look like when constructed, I imagined a stomach, postpartum, like a crushed red vegetable. Attempting nevertheless to remain cheerful, I decided the next day to call school.

Christina was surprised to hear from me and asked, after a pause, how I had been. I told her that I'd been great and suggested that perhaps I might visit in April. "Well," Christina said, "you know there are big exams in April, and we'll probably go to Florida for spring break. You know, also, I pushed the beds together, so where would you sleep?"

My father walked into the room. "When you get off, call Stein—immediately. We move on the discovery clause now."

Christina said, "Look, we're headed out to the Rat for happy hour. So, maybe I'll see ya again, okay?" and hung up.

I sat there for a moment wanting to cry, then dialed Mr.

Stein's office. Before he could ask, I said that I was great. Then I said, "Leave the files open, okay? Just leave me alone," and dropped the phone, Mr. Stein's voice still asking, "You're sure now?"

I turned to find my father still by the door. "One more thing," he said. "You're not by law supposed to see the child, but your mother and I want to arrange . . ." and I shouted, "I don't want to see it! You were eavesdropping, you heard what I said: Just leave me alone!"

On March 30 I woke up at 2:00 A.M. feeling as if I'd been kicked in the side. My mother said, "Oh, sweetheart," and left to call Dr. Goldberg. Ten minutes later she walked back in with my father. "Okay, babe," he said, "tomorrow morning at nine — just another seven hours."

My parents went to bed but left the doors to our rooms open because, as my father explained, "Every time there is a pregnant woman in this house, we leave the doors open." I turned on the TV and leaned back horizontally across the beanbag, wondering what other pregnant women he was talking about.

At 2:15 A.M. I focused on *Getting Straight,* a movie about sixties radicals who must decide whether they will become middle-class or stay with the fight. I realized as I watched that even if I survived this experience, life might not prove to be all that interesting. The college girls of 1977 — the girls I'd be surrounded by for years — were not concerned with social change. They preferred to destroy people through gossip. When not decimating one of their peers, they were stoned. I picked up my notebook at 3:00 A.M. to record an insight. *My pregnancy,* I wrote, was not in fact that at all. It was *merely a metaphor for the age — like disco.*

The sky at 6:00 A.M. was as flat, as speckled gray as a slice of cardboard. I lay shivering in the beanbag, wondering what to bring and what would happen to me once I got there. My mother came in and I asked her. "Just bring yourself," she said, "and as far as what to expect, well," and went on to list several things. It sounded terrible. I said, "Forget it."

The ride up 135 passed more quickly than I'd remembered. I concentrated on the pains that pricked my side, hoping to ignore the hospital, a mirage of beige brick that rose up on the right like a prison amid split-levels. But almost immediately, it seemed, we were there. I tried to stall for time. I asked about the nurses: What if one of them had gone to Tremor? And what had Dr. Goldberg said about Dr. Leonard, the baby doctor—something about him doing "the prenatal"? My mother said, "Let's just get in there, okay?"

We walked across the parking lot between ambulances, stretchers hanging out the backs like white tongues. Grabbing my mother's hand, I said, "I guess I'm sick now, aren't I?"

E I G H T

In the admissions office a middle-aged blond woman looked at me and promptly pointed to a chair. "Sit there," she ordered as she led my mother aside.

"Look," she whispered loudly, "you'll have to sign for her.

Despite her, well, her situation, she is still underage."

"I am not," I said, standing. "I am eighteen, and you can ask me whatever questions you have."

"You sit down in that chair and mind your business," she snapped, offering my mother a raised-eyebrow sigh.

My mother did not sigh in return. "My daughter is eighteen years of age," she said crisply. "Don't you treat her like a child, she will sign for herself. I'll wait outside."

After several questions about what exactly I was signing and a few threats on the woman's part to "alert staff" to my attitude, a wheelchair appeared and I was placed into it, legs flying straight out in front. I wore a baggy blue-striped dress from eleventh grade and a pair of old clogs over Gwyn's yellow Snoopy knee socks. I held a suede purse trimmed with fringe. My hair was in a ponytail. People sitting in the lobby followed my progress across. I covered my face.

Riding up in the elevator, I decided to take another approach: I would appear polite and eager. I smiled at everyone, seeming for two or three minutes very happy to be sitting there among them. Then the doors opened and the chair plunged at high speed into a green-walled maze, whipping around corners, dodging stretchers draped with sheets and machines with steel drills like a dentist's. Out of the green ahead loomed dark tiny rooms and, beyond them to the right, a vast glassed-in cage like an aquarium. Someone in the distance screamed. When the chair came to a stop, I almost fell out.

I was left standing in a long dirty pink room. Torn gray shower curtains separated two beds from a small area at the front, where several dentist's machines had been assembled. Three male doctors stood over a woman in the second bed. I wondered about these machines, stopped myself, and wondered if the woman next to me was young, perhaps my age, for the men were speaking in falsetto voices, murmuring

"Okay, honey," as if she were a child. I wondered next what she was doing there at all: Mr. Stein was supposed to have arranged for a private room. I felt my pulse quicken. The pains were back. My mother came in.

"What is this?" I asked, nodding at the woman who lay next to me. "There isn't supposed to be anybody else here." My mother said, "Hold on," and walked off to investigate, only to be led back by a thin, brittle-haired blonde wearing stained green sheets like a poncho. The room seemed to swell with ammonia.

"Say bye-bye," cooed the nurse, grabbing at my bag, "and take this lovely item with you."

I asked the nurse if I could please, for security's sake, keep my bag. She ran gravel-gray eyes over me, smirked and said, "I don't want one bit of trouble from you, do you understand me? I've had one hell of a night. And your mother, for the record, can't stay. It's against regulations. Got it?"

I nodded, folded my arms and started to cry. My mother shook the nurse free. "Good luck, sweetheart," she said, taking the bag. "I'll talk to you soon." The nurse escorted her out, then returned in a trail of ammonia.

"Your mother tells me you don't know where you are," she said, placing one hand at a time on each hip. "I guess that's a bit of an understatement, isn't it?"

She looked tired. Puffy half-moons of skin sagged beneath each eye. I tried to be polite. "I was supposed to have a private room," I said, trying to read her crooked name tag. "How come there's another bed here?"

The nurse turned and began to line up needles on a tray. "This is the labor room, sweetheart. Now get those clothes off, everything, put it in here." She tossed me a paper bag, a piece of green fabric she called a gown, and parted the shower curtain to make way for the other woman, who was moaning, "Jesus P. Christ," and was not, I saw, my age at all.

As the ammonia nurse walked out with the crowd, another looking remarkably like her came in.

"Okay now," chirped the new nurse. "Let's get those panties off—and up on the table. I'll be back in a jiffy to shave you." This made me think of a porn movie I'd seen in the city while cutting school once senior year. I tried to get her to be as specific as possible.

"I beg your pardon," I said politely, "what was I supposed to do?"

"I told you, honey," she said loudly, "up on that table, spread those legs and I'll be back with the razor, okay?"

Standing there, awaiting the razor, I tried to seem casual. I thought of Dhani: If he were here, what would he say? He would say, "Be conscious of your environment," of course. I studied the walls, which were a sort of salmon color, the color you might end up with if you painted pink over lima bean green. I listened to girls screaming somewhere nearby. I had heard these high-pitched shrieks before, but only on the news and coming usually from Arab women whose villages had recently burned. I decided to forget my environment. I would not look at the dentist instruments of death. I would be brave. With fingers in my ears, I looked up at the clock: 9:30. The girls at school would be on line at Erie Dining Hall.

At 9:32 they were back—the ammonia nurse, who'd straightened her name tag so that I could read the word *Bacon;* the chirpy nurse with the razor, plus several others in matching sheet outfits, none with name tags. I asked about Dr. Goldberg, but they would not answer. "He was supposed to meet me here," I explained. "When is he coming? Can you tell me?"

"Not now, honey," one of them called over her shoulder. "Now get your behind *carefully* up on that table."

"I have to talk to him," I said, "there's been a mistake,"

but they were rushing around the room, fast and blurry as a bee swarm, and would not answer. "Please," I said, "Miss Bacon, will you tell me where he is?" But she said nothing. "Hey," I called, jumping rear end first onto the table. Two bees raced right over. "Honey, where the hell do you think you are, gym class?" one asked. Lowering me by a shoulder, Nurse Bacon added, "I am in no mood for this crap!"

They gathered solemnly to watch the chirpy's work, the room silent except for water dripping somewhere onto tin. Gradually I recognized this as the clicking sound of Nurse Bacon's tongue. "Voilà," said the chirpy when she'd finished. "Very nice," said Nurse Bacon, pushing her way through the crowd. "Now, let's get on with it." Framed between my knees, she whipped open a glove and shoved her hand so far up inside me I pictured her grabbing my heart. Looking down at me, she ordered, "Breathe."

"But I am breathing," I said.

"This is just what I'm talking about," she said through clenched teeth. "Come on, will someone hold her still? I am not going to put up with this."

"I'm sorry," I gasped. "I'll breathe better."

But Nurse Bacon would accept no apology. She removed the hand, walked to my side and proceeded to jab a finger into the area corresponding roughly to my bladder. I could not help myself, I screamed, and a new nurse appeared with a needle. Nurse Bacon retreated, whispering, "Sixteen, it's outrageous." I was about to say, "Eighteen," but the new nurse was rolling me away toward the wall. As she rolled me back, I saw the head nurse select a needle of her own. I thought quickly of something to calm her.

"I had a pregnancy test," I said. "It came out negative"— the same story I'd tried on Steve in the summer, only updated. Nurse Bacon's eyes seemed to soften. Not only was I a teenager, but I was a victim of the U.S. health-care system!

Just as I thought we were friends, coworkers at least, she rolled me around, held back my right arm and jammed a needle the size of a skewer through my ass.

"What's the deal with the contractions?" she barked. "When did they start? What about the water?"

"What water?" I asked as the bee swarm flew around the room. "What water are you talking about?" But the needle, some kind of sedative, had acted with the one before to slow things down. The walls had become wavy, scalloped and pink, as things seemed while tripping. Darting bees left trails behind them in the air, what looked like long, slimy streaks of flying vomit. Voices reached me—roll over, keep those legs apart, stop babbling—but it was confusing and hard to move. My head ached. My lower body had become a dull, thick block of pain I could imagine detached, an ejector rocket cut off from the craft. I wanted to get up but had never felt heavier. I tried at least to keep my eyes open.

I focused at one point on a tiny oriental woman dressed in white. She took my arm and started massaging it, poking gently at the veins. I thought of the shiatsu treatment Dhani had spoken of. When she asked me to turn my head toward the wall, to think about ice cream and cookies, I recalled the "visualization" technique that accompanied it. I pictured Good Humor, toasted almond on a stick, alongside an Oreo. The woman proceeded to jam what felt like a spear inside my arm, cutting through, it seemed, to the elbow.

Moving my head back into place, she said, "My God, look at those stretch marks! Like a regular tattooed lady. I guess you won't be wearing a bikini this summer, honey, will you?" I told her, trying to laugh with the others, that it wasn't the most important thing to consider right now. What I thought was, Fucking bitch. Then the anesthesia kicked in.

The world from then on seemed tight and dark, as if someone had wrapped me in a blanket and gripped my body with a vise. I thought of The Mummy and realized that I'd made a pun, but couldn't quite remember the difference between a pun and a bad joke. I wondered where the nurses had gone so suddenly and how much time had elapsed since the shot. I could say for sure that I was still in the labor room, which still had the sickly sour smell of a hamster cage. But Dr. Goldberg had not come, nor had my mother returned with my purse. And I had no idea what they'd do next. I'd try to sit up, find that I could not and then just lie there.

I awoke hours later to find that I'd been attached by thick tentacles to a beeping brown tank. I heard one bee say, "The fetal monitor." Another one said, "Dr. Leonard, the prenatal." I tried to explain that Dr. Leonard could not see me. I shaped my lips to say no, but received another shot and said nothing. When I looked up next one bee stood over me, smiling. Dr. Leonard, I sensed, had come and gone. Then, from the corridor outside, I heard the other doctor, Dr. Goldberg, and with a bee on either side he stepped in at last to untie me from the beeping brown tank and, I hoped, to fire the nurses. I asked him what time it was. He said, "Eleven o'clock in the P.M." I asked him if we could have the lights on. He laughed and said, "Okay, baby. Here we go."

Someone focused a spotlight above my head, and four bees held me down. "This'll pinch," said my doctor, sticking a finger with a long nail or else a knife between my legs. "Breathe, baby," he growled. "Breathe, goddammit," hissed Nurse Bacon, whose face looked made of wax. But breathing to me seemed impossible. I said, "Please stop." The doctor's arm came out. I exhaled. "Now get a grip," he said, and he aimed and delivered one final jab, the pain shooting far up into my head as gallons of fluid, some kind of stream, came rushing out. I threw up, then asked, "Did I have it?" Everyone laughed and the table I was on turned in circles. A black man wheeled me out, although I wasn't yet asleep. I wanted someone to notice. But I could only watch the blur of slippery pink tile as it turned to green, the way the ocean, if you walk too far out, turns from blue to black, which reminded me I had a bruise on my arm, but there was no time to examine it. We were on the elevator heading down. The black man said, "Your time has come, little mama," and the doors opened. Nurse Bacon was waiting.

When I woke up again I was lying on a stretcher in a hallway. There was a nurse in white above me saying something about a "serious suction." I asked her what time it was. She said, "Three-fifteen." I asked her what day and she said, "April Fools. You're all emptied out." I put a hand to my stomach. It was indeed empty, wiggling beneath the sheets like mint jelly. I tried to smile. I wanted to ask if it had been a girl, but suddenly I was in a bed in a room by myself, looking out at several doors. One led to the outside world, I supposed, and one was most likely a closet with a mirror on the back. There was a dark smear in the glass that might have been me, but someone snuck up with a needle. I fell asleep.

When I woke up next it was morning. My mother was sitting at the side of my bed wearing a trench coat.

The baby, she said without my asking, was a girl—a very large one, which partially accounted for my weight gain. At one point, she explained, this very big baby had tangled dangerously with her cord: The heartbeat had grown weaker; Goldberg had called them to consult. Reviewing the options, they had agreed to a cesarean section, which would leave a vertical scar in addition, she was afraid, to other scars. "Your weight gain was extreme," she said, pausing for breath. "Fifty pounds, sweetheart. He told you to go easy on the food. I'm afraid there may be some scarring, okay?"

It was not okay, nor was this story recited too quickly. I felt hugely embarrassed that I did not know it already; it was, after all, about my body. But each time I tried to ask how Goldberg had dared consult them and not me, no sound came out. My mother, removing gluey strands of hair from my cheek, said, "Well, sweetheart," and got up. She placed on the bed a crossword puzzle book, some underwear, a new bathrobe and my suede purse so that I wouldn't feel "out of touch with the world." She floated out, saying, "Daddy will be by soon."

It was dark the next time I woke up. There was a television on and a nurse puncturing the one remaining flat spot of my buttock. When she was through I guided my hand to the spot to see if there were lumps. Just as I had fixed one hand on a welt, in walked my father. "Bees," I explained. He nodded, set down a plant and a notebook, then began nervously, as my mother had, to speak. The baby's head, he said, had been improperly positioned. The umbilical cord had practically wrapped itself around the neck, and so a cesarean had been performed, general anesthesia administered, powerful painkillers used as backup. Some words formed and fell off my lips. "Why am I hearing all of this from you?" I croaked.

"Because you should know," he said, "you should know what happened and know what to expect as a result. The child's body weight totaled more than eight pounds. I've been led to believe there may be some scarring as a result."

I tried to say that this wasn't the explanation I wanted, but could not arrange the words. I sat there in silence. My father finished his speech and studied a bad painting of the Mediterranean Sea that hung above my bed. He discussed the colors found only in that part of the world. At last two bees came in and said, "Bye-bye time." My father formally handed me the notebook. "When you are able, write everything down. It's important that you remember what has happened. Do you understand me?"

I nodded, dropped it and let one of the bees give me a shot.

The next day, I was slightly more coherent to greet Gwyn, who arrived early with flowers. She stood at the foot of my bed and asked how I was. I said, trying to flip back my hair, that I was relieved and went on to lie about how great, physically, I felt.

Gwyn removed a brush from her macramé purse. "You look like total shit. Just let me comb it a little, okay?"

I closed my eyes as she worked, pretending that she was teasing it, arranging it specially for some kind of date. "What is in this hair?" she asked, searching unsuccessfully for a part. "It's like varnish." Still in my fantasy, I shrugged. Gwyn sighed and stepped back. "I don't think we're going to get it all clean right now," she said, "but I'll put some blush on you so you'll at least feel more human." Dreamily I watched her take out a compact and, with a finger, rub the liquid red into my cheek. Holding up a mirror, she said, "Gorgeous." I remembered suddenly where we were, the bizarre circumstance of this combing. I slapped the mirror to the floor.

My mother walked in and picked it up. Handing it to Gwyn, smiling, she said, "Well, *I* see an improvement."

I tried to think of something to say in response. I said, "What about Steve?"

My mother told me that she had called him and that he'd said, "It's all over? Good."

"That's it?" I asked.

"I'm afraid so," she said.

I was too exhausted to say much more. Conserving my

strength, I waited, then asked why Steve hadn't called.

My mother sighed. "Honey, it's because he went to Florida for spring break, remember?"

I remembered encouraging him to go, not wanting him around the hospital attracting the secretaries and Rainbo. I thought about how depressed he had been and told myself that Steve needed a vacation. I also thought that if he died while traveling it would not be the worst possible thing. The phone rang.

"Don't you want to pick it up, sweetie?" asked my mother. I said that I did not. "Well," she said, nodding at the phone, "do you want me to pick it up?" I said no, and so we sat there, the phone ringing, until at last a bee came thrashing in to answer.

"It's your adoption attorney," she said, handing me the receiver. The nurse smirked at my mother. My mother frowned at her, blew kisses at me and left with Gwyn. I picked up to hear Mr. Stein say, "Hey, babe." Inhaling, he added, "You've been out like a light. But I hear from reliable sources that you're doing just great. Holding up beautifully."

"The nurses," I whispered, "are trying to kill me."

Mr. Stein promised to see what could be done just as soon as I'd told him exactly how I was feeling "about, you know, just everything! How about, let's say, emotionally, first. No regrets?"

I whispered, "The nurses are trying to kill me. You must do something—please!"

Mr. Stein said, "You calm right down. I'll investigate and get back for our heart-to-heart ASAP."

The phone rang ten minutes later, and I picked up to hear what he'd worked out. But it was Sashi. She was crying because, as she explained, "They said I'm only ten and can't come see you." I said, "You're not missing anything." She

said, "Well, I guess I *can* come with Daddy to get you and
the, uh, I mean to get *you.* "

I felt a chill, the first physical sensation below the neck I'd
had in days. "Fine, Sashi," I said, "but I'm expecting a call. I
have to go now." For three hours I stared at the phone. It
never rang.

The next night my parents arrived from Nanny Etta's Seder
loaded down with half a chicken, a honey cake, a rubber plant
with "care and feeding" instructions from Etta, plus a
handwritten list of things I should do to fight mono from my
grandfather and, from my grandmother Florita, a special
Christian Science message. My father, inspired perhaps by the
Mediterranean Sea painting, discussed the origin of the sea
chanty. My mother tried to make me eat. In the midst of the
festivities, Dr. Goldberg called to say that I could leave in
two days, on April 6. My father interrupted his discourse to
say, "You're almost home." I tried to smile, noticed that my
lips had badly cracked, and began to eat the challah, the
kugel, the potato salad, as quickly as my mother could get it
out onto the bed.

When they'd gone home, I flipped through a *Glamour*
magazine Gwyn had dropped the day before as she left. It
seemed that I was moving my lips as I read, as if translating
from another language. I remembered my fears about brain
damage, panicked and let the magazine fall. A black woman
in a striped dress walked in and picked it up. Tossing it onto
a chair, she said, "What are you doing lying there like that?
We did you days ago, let's move that hiney out of bed. Let's
go. We're gonna get you cleaned up."

I said, "A cesarean, please, leave me," but she seemed not
to hear. She was pulling my legs over the side of the bed and

trying to grab one of my hands. "Please, no," I said as she scooped her hand beneath my ass. "Stop it!" I shrieked. "Get your hands off me!"

"Oh, my goodness," she said, stepping back. "Did you have a section? Why didn't you say so? Let me help you."

"Leave this room now," I said, "or I will call the police. Get out now. Get out." Two bee reinforcements arrived at the door. One walked off with the black girl, who called, "I'm sorry, God," over her shoulder. One remained. Imitating a little girl, she said, "I think it's about time for your enema."

It was raining when she left, but I did not dare call her back to close the window. I fell asleep shivering in wet wind and woke up the next morning in tears. The tears quickly turned to sobs, and I lay there holding my stomach, afraid that it would tear apart if I let go. I could hear the nurses wheeling babies to their mothers for feeding and thought for the first time about my own, about how it was all alone, with nothing to look at but green or pink walls, getting its food from the cunt killer bees, if they bothered to feed it. Nobody —my goddamned father included—asked me about it now; they were hoping I would forget.

I cried for a while, then called Mr. Stein to say that I wanted to see it, despite what I'd told my father that day, despite whatever law said I couldn't. He rushed me off the phone. Five minutes later I picked up to hear my mother talking: She'd had an emergency call from Goldberg, who'd heard from Stein, and what was this about seeing the baby? What was going on? Had I had a change of feeling? What was all this about? I told her the only thing I felt like was Rosemary, mother of the devil, and hung up. I knew then that I would have to find the baby by myself, without Stein or Goldberg or my parents, without anyone who called me "babe."

Breathing evenly, I lifted myself up onto my elbows and

swung one leg over the side of the bed. Positioned for action, I discovered that I could not move one inch either way. I lay there on my elbows, the leg dangling, until a bee appeared with a wheelchair. "Let's go," she said, moving the other leg off the bed. "We're giving you five minutes."

We parked outside the aquarium window, and I watched as a bee wearing a green mask carried a large plastic container toward the glass. She came to a stop and tilted it. Inside, a tiny, black-eyed baby stretched and yawned but did not look directly at me. I tried to think of the appropriate thing to say. I could not think of it. I tried to determine whether or not the baby looked like me. I couldn't tell. It was best, I decided, not to think but to wait, seated, until I felt overwhelmed with emotion and had to move. When nothing happened, I tried to conjure up some feeling, some behavior —shifting my head, saying "oooh"—that I associated with mothers and babies. But the only thing I felt for sure was exhaustion. The bee behind the glass nodded and the basket vanished.

The phone was ringing back in my room, and I picked it up to tell Mr. Stein that no, I hadn't changed my mind. Mr. Stein exhaled. I started crying. "Go on," he said, "talk it through—talk about the baby."

I said, "My fucking friends betrayed me. How can I go back to that hell? I have no place."

"Forget about them," he said. "You've had an experience they'll most likely never have. Now that's something, isn't it?" When I did not respond, he added, "Look at it this way: You're almost back home, and you're in great physical shape!"

That night Dr. Goldberg came in to change the bandage. Removing shears from his white coat pocket, he said, "Baby, I don't want you to be upset." He sliced through layers of gauze, mumbling, "Hang on." He pulled the old tape off a little too quickly and said, "Okay, you can look."

Focusing on the spot, I opened my eyes to slits, the way I kept them watching horror films late at night on TV. Dr. Goldberg was blotting brown blood from a dark purple incision laced up with black thread. Two thick pouches of skin like pleated drapes hung from either side of the scar. There were stretch marks as wide and as long as thumbs. I saw no belly button.

"Baby," Dr. Goldberg said as tears rolled into my ears, "I told you to lay off the food."

The sun slashed the bed at 6:00 A.M. the next day, and I woke up scared: of the nurses who might notice I had yet to walk and make me stay; of getting back through the lobby; of going home. I could not remember what I'd put on my list of things to do in the future. I could not quite remember if I'd done something so dumb as to make a list.

I stood two hours later in my blue-striped dress, pulling at the damp, wrinkly material by the waist. My mother walked in, watched me and asked, "How's the scar?"

Swallowing, I said, "Oh, it's fine, nothing too bad."

"Well," she said as a wheelchair was parked by the door, "that's some relief. I'll just go check last-minute things."

"It's fine, really," I said as she walked out. Collapsing into the chair, I said, more truthfully, "It's a mess." I said this again as someone, my mother, I assumed, came up behind me. "Ma?" I called, too tired to get up.

"No," said a deep voice, "it's not Ma." I smelled the ammonia and tried to wheel the chair across the room, but Nurse Bacon gripped the handles. Leaning down, she kissed the top of my head. "Next time, sweetheart," she whispered, "be more careful."

There was an official procession, according to rules: One green-sheeted nurse pushed the chair; my mother walked on my right, a nurse in white on the left. We stopped at the aquarium and others joined in—an entire rear flank of nurses surrounding the baby, who started seconds later to cry. One of the bees made *oooh* sounds and I wanted to scream, Get your hands off my baby, you bitch, but Mr. Stein appeared, shouting about the couple—"ecstatically waiting on the other side of the parking lot for delivery!"—and then we came out into the lobby.

My mother helped me into the car, which had been parked out front. Someone else handed me the blob of blankets, which, according to arcane law or for the lunchtime entertainment of the nurses, I'd have to physically "give up" to a social worker. The baby had been wrapped like a present—every inch covered, all corners neatly tucked. My mind roamed for a minute to suffocation. It roamed next to "I Love Lucy," to the episode in which Lucy pretends that a cheese in a blanket is a baby: not a pun, I almost shouted, but a thick, empty joke. Sashi leaned over the seat. "Look how cute," she said, pulling back a blanket corner, and my mother said, "Yes." I looked at my father, who bit his lower lip. I looked down. The baby looked up and started crying.

Two social workers stood on the curb cheering. "Come on, girl," they were saying, as if calling a dog, "there ya go," and I watched as their arms filled the car. Hands clamped on to the blankets. There was a tug. Someone called "Touchdown!" and the door slammed as I raised one hand to the windshield.

"Are you all right?" my father asked me.

"Yeah," I told him, the April heat burning like an iron on my cheek, "we'll see, I mean," and we drove home.

NINE

I limped, my first day home, as far as the mirror. Wrapping my fingers around an old white lipstick, I wrote *I Lived* on the antique glass, then passed out. On the second day I wrote this again, in script, then tried slowly to dress. One hour later, wearing a pair of my father's old corduroy pants held up by suspenders, a sweatshirt and sunglasses, I walked down to find my family seated at the kitchen table, as if they'd rehearsed.

"Here she is," said my mother. Sashi said, "Yay." Gwyn said, "You're wearing my sunglasses, but that's okay." My father stared. "How are you, babe?" he whispered after everyone had spoken. "Tell us of your feelings." My strongest feeling was embarrassment. They were staring at me. It was regarding something gynecological. Avoiding my father's eyes, I said, "I'm totally fine. It's over. How else should I feel?" and walked slowly back upstairs to sit by the phone.

I decided after a while to dial whatever number came into my head, beginning with Val's, which I'd known longest. The Gnome answered, informed me that Val was living with Victor, said she could not recall their number and hung up. Next, Caro Carroway's mother said, "She went with Rainbo to drive Cyndi Fein, who's moving to Israel, to the airport. Then they're going to visit Jason at his school." I realized as she spoke that I was still quite high from all the shots. The effort of dialing the phone had proved exhausting, the thought of reentering a world that had in it Cyndi Fein and Rainbo even more so.

Hoping my head wouldn't drop, I said, "Tell Caro I'm better now," walked past my father and back to my room to lie down. I woke up the following day in the same outfit. The stitches, my mother was saying as she shook me, were due to come out.

After I had waited two hours, Dr. Goldberg patted my head, chuckled and said, "What a little fatty you are now." Snipping black threads, he added, "I'm going to give you some pills, but in August we'll get you fixed up with an IUD. I don't think we want to trust you permanently with the Pill." He offered his final thoughts. "Thanks to the cesarean," he said, tossing a plastic glove into the trash, "you're practically a virgin."

I sat up all night, afraid that I'd burst awake, see the scars and start to scream. In the morning I dressed with the lights off and curtains closed. Then I walked down the block to meet Steve, despite the way my father followed me across the lawn shouting, "Stay away from that car." Steve, home on Easter break, drove too fast, pointing out the possible restaurants we could go to, as he had promised. I said that each one looked nice. At some point I said, "Steve, I have to break up with you."

Steve slammed on the brakes. "You'll change your mind, babe," he said, giving the finger to some guy behind us, "you're just in shock."

"No," I said as he hit the gas, "there isn't anything left. It's a high school romance that got *severely* carried away. Now I need time to myself. I have to get my head completely together before I go back to school."

"You can get your head together with me," Steve said, pinching my knee.

"Steve," I said, closing my eyes, "please don't give me a hard time—and please take your hand off my knee. Look, I have to break up and that's it."

"You'll change your mind," he mumbled as we turned onto the Southern State Parkway. "We've been through some heavy shit, babe. There's no gettin' out of it."

I put my fingers in my ears and watched the road. Bushes heavy with pink and white blossoms drooped over fences like quilts out to be aired. "It is finally spring," I whispered. "You lived." But Steve was driving faster, hitting bumps straight on so that I had to hold the loose pouch of skin, formerly the blob, with one hand.

Three days back out in the world proved overwhelming. I woke up on the fourth feeling dizzy. At breakfast I dropped my cereal spoon, watched the raisin bran turn to milky swamp and walked back up the stairs to my room. I looked at myself in the mirror—from the side, from the back, from the side—then lay on the bed and started sobbing. My mother, whispering first to my father, came in to hold my head in her lap.

"Sweetheart," she said, smoothing out my hair. "Every woman suffers some kind of postpartum depression. It's to be expected."

This reminded me of her speech years ago before the Betty movie. It was interesting enough, no doubt biologically correct. It did not, however, seem to have very much to do with my individual situation.

"Are you thinking about the baby?" she asked.

I looked at her. "Ma," I sobbed, "I'm thinking about *me*. My life is over. What do *I* have?"

At her suggestion I constructed a list: I was not in school, as were my former roommates and a few friends. I had no job. I had no boyfriend. I had no money and nothing to do except read. And though I didn't put it on the list I made for my mother, I had also ruined my body for life, which meant I probably wouldn't have another boyfriend. Getting up a while later I noticed that I had bled through onto my father's pants. My mother noticed too and, without mentioning it, said, "Why don't you go pants shopping? I'll drive you to the mall, and then you can walk home and begin to think all these things through."

Coming out of The Gap later that afternoon, I ran straight into Karen and Debbie, the secretarial-girl detectives. Their eyes scanned the range from stomach to face at such high speed, I almost fell over. "Hi," I said, "I am just home from school for vacation." But they were riveted by my waist, their mouths cranked open as if they'd rusted that way the night at Johnny Mac's. "Well, gotta go," I said. Karen crossed her arms; Debbie's mouth widened to form a crevice on the lower half of her face.

On the mirror at home I put a white question mark after the words *I Lived,* then crossed it out. Opening my notebook, I wrote, *I must believe that school, the future, is only 25 weeks away: back to Calverton to finish what I started so well! The past already seems like a million years ago. Who can believe it's only a week?*

Toward the middle of April I realized that the drugs, the hundred or so shots of Nurse Bacon, were wearing off. Quick pains shot through my thighs. My stomach itched, though like a flabby cheek numb with novocaine, it could be scratched for hours without relief. Poking, rubbing, practically tearing at my skin, I decided as a first step back to normal life that I would look.

The thin brown line had faded to a strip of clotted tan, but the stretch marks remained—in the form of red gashes on my stomach and sides and white indentations, like tiny paw prints, on my thighs. Staring at them, smearing liquid foundation over 70 percent of my body, I felt a slow panic settle in, steady as a TV test pattern. It was hot in my room. It was April 15 or near it, which meant that soon it would be summer, which meant summer clothes. Wiping off the makeup, I decided to concentrate on what I'd wear.

I spent hours and then days transforming clip-on turtlenecks and tube tops into girdles. I designed clever midriff flaps for old halters and cut the sleeves to make tank tops out of leotards. But studying my creations in the mirror, I'd see only a piece of fabric sinking into the folds of skin at my waist. I'd stare at it for so long my father would shout, "Where's Betsy?" One sister would walk in to see. I'd scream, "Can't I be alone?" This went on three days. On the fourth, to my relief, a friend of the family's turned up a full-time summer job for me—as an assistant at a Farmingdale book depository. Settling on sleeveless cotton blouses and long denim skirts, avoiding my father, who seemed to follow me around, I went out for the first time to drive: to preregister for summer school; to the library, where I planned to check out books alphabetically from A onward; and then later that night to eat with Caro.

We sat talking for hours in the Nautilus Diner. Caro told me that Val had become a private secretary; that Rainbo had "gone Buddhist"; that she herself was attending community college. She also told me—"just 'cuz you should know"—that people had spent the winter gossiping about how I was probably pregnant.

"What a lot of stories about one kid," she said, blowing smoke out over jelly-streaked plates into my face.

Wiping up the coffee I'd spilled when my wrist jerked, I said, "Oh, you know, I gained weight at school. It's typical."

"Yeah, I noticed you gained it," Caro said. "You know, like everyone I had my suspicions, like when you came in that time. But," she assured me, biting a cold french fry in half, "it didn't seem like something you'd get into."

Minutes passed. Caro waved a hand in front of my face. "Well, don't get upset about it," she said, sounding surprised. "People have to talk about something. You know how it is around here."

I leaned back to peel the skin pouch, like a large fleshy slug, from my thigh. I said, "I'm tired, Caro. I think I'll just go home."

Sitting later that night in the beanbag, I heard two things that would come to define the summer now only several weeks away: the first was a call at 3:00 A.M. in which the caller hung up as my father answered; the second was a radio report of a murder—two kids had been shot and killed with a

.44 handgun as they sat in a parked car in the Bronx. The attack was similar to five others during the past year. This time, however, the killer—who called himself Samantha— had left a note. I turned off the radio and fell asleep in the chair, dreaming that I sat in a car parked by Zappa watching a man in black walk slowly toward me. Smashing the windshield, he took my hand, sliced it with a knife, then drew a gun.

As an employee of the Jepson Book Company, I sat in a corner office of the Audio-Visual Department with Mrs. Miriam Snee, a short, busty lady who had a slight graying mustache and a phlegmy throat. It was my job to copy down information from brochures describing educational filmstrips. Out the window I had a view of a Jewish cemetery. Occasionally I turned to catch Miriam picking her nose with the eraser end of a pencil. I stared at my watch: At 10:20 there was a coffee break; at 10:24, a "return" bell; at 12:25, lunch. I sat at lunch with Brillo-haired ladies who made little piles of lipstick-kiss cigarette butts in cups. I'd reflect on how if I'd been high the filters might have looked like broken candy canes. Then I'd excuse myself to read in the far bathroom stall.

In my purse I kept the alphabetical book of the week and several ladies' magazines I'd bought in search of stretch-mark cures. I found an ad one day—"Hi-Potency E Toner!! Gets rid of strech marks that ugly red forever!!"—and stuffed it, with five dollars, into a Jepson envelope I labeled *Emergency*. I read in another ad about the regenerative properties of the aloe plant and spent an evening in the skin-cream aisle of Genovese Drugs. *Hope at last!* I wrote after rubbing white lotion all over my body. But the Hi-Potency E Toner never arrived. The only change due to aloe was the way Miriam would look at me, puzzled, after lunch and say, "Why, dear, you've grease marks on your blouse." I'd smile at her, eat half a leftover codeine tab, horrified to find that it was only 1:05 out of a possible 5:13, when, groggy and hot, I'd drive home in my mother's car at the end of a long, thin trail of traffic. The car's AM radio would not hold stations. I'd finally find a song that I liked—by the Beatles or maybe one from seventh grade—and it would fade, blurring, as the car inched slowly forward, with newer songs and, on most nights, screeching static.

When Steve returned from school in late May, he called and said, "You at least have to let me take you to the restaurant like I promised." Considering my job, my body and my social life, I said, "Okay, Steve. Just for the night," and suggested that we meet at the Plankhouse, the expensive date place in a corner of the old White's parking lot.

The owners of the Plankhouse had apparently "gone disco," replacing the wooden booths with wavy white-rock modules you had to step into, so that you ate tucked inside a sort of large stucco egg. I stepped into ours, ordered a pink-and-green drink—"just like a Slurpee," explained the waitress—and removed Steve's hand from my thigh. Steve stared at me, replaced the hand and, without blinking, spoke in a monotone: about how he planned to work in June and early July with Mickey in New Jersey, about how, before then, we would go jogging and on vacation to Fire Island and about what bathing suit I'd wear. Displacing the hand, I studied the dates unfolding within the modules around me. All too easily, I thought, I could have ended up like the secretary with the air-brushed bangs and faded Huk-A-Poo shirt one egg over. But the class distinction between us was not quite clear. All we'd have to do, I thought, was pull up our shirts and compare, but the drinks came, Steve's hand again made progress up my leg, and I told myself to forget it.

Steve did not stop talking once throughout the entire meal. Slowly it occurred to me that this was strange. Outside in the car, I said, "Steve, why are you acting so weird? I can't stay with you. We've gone through this."

Steve said, "You'll have to change your mind," and leaned toward me with his tongue out. Chills rushed even to the numb part of my waist.

"Steve," I said, pushing him away, "you have got to get a grip on reality."

"I'd like to get a grip on you, babe."

"This is it," I said. "I'm walking. You disgust me."

Steve grabbed at my stomach. "Who else are you gonna show that to?" he shouted. "You wanna streak through a bar and see how many guys follow you out? Be my guest." He sighed and flipped on the radio. I opened my door, heard the words "forty-four-caliber killer" and closed it.

"What have you heard about Samantha?" I asked. Steve turned up the volume and smirked.

"Not Samantha," he whispered, grabbing now at my breast, "it's *Son of Sam.*" I pushed him away, got out and ran. Steve started the car and followed. "You'll be fucking sorry," he shrieked before driving off the other way.

Slowing my pace, I worried about the Son of Sam. I considered the overwhelming coincidence that the female victims were all my age with long brown hair. I considered this fact again when the phone rang that night at 3:00 A.M. Although the killings had gone on for one year, it seemed possible to me at that moment that the Son of Sam might be Steve.

Son of Sam quickly became the most talked about person on Long Island. Not since Beatlemania or the controversial "Clic-Clacs" toy—two glass balls on a string that had once made the cover of *Newsday*—had there been one common thread of conversation. I'd hear from a cashier that he drove a yellow van and killed women who looked like his mother— brunettes with shoulder-length hair or longer, although shags, Gwyn would say as we drove to the mall, slouched, were thought okay.

Everyone had their theories: Son of Sam was an imperfect anagram for Manson, or else it stood for S & M and was the pseudonym of a businessman rapist who drove a red VW out from midtown. I myself suspected Steve. Driving around, one hand covering the side of my head, I'd say, "It's ridiculous. You're getting fears confused. Besides, he's in New Jersey." Still, I spent considerable time matching Steve's actions to Sam's: On June 6 the police made public a letter Sam had written to a columnist; I searched the papers for a handwriting sample. On June 26 Sam shot and wounded two in Bayside, Queens, and I called Steve's house and then Mickey's, just to see if he was there or sounded guilty. But he did not answer the phone in either place and I hung up. I did not find samples of Sam's writing. Fear spread.

On July 1 my father gathered our family to warn, "You are to survey the road at all times." Stopped at a light July 2, Rainbo shouted from behind newly yellow hair, "I'd dye it, Israel, or you'll die," and I said, "Fuck," as I drove, lifting the pouch of skin from my thigh and shifting lanes—for red VWs, for men with white hair—peering into cars on either side of the traffic trail. Girls peered back, hunched in their seats, dark hair pinned up, dark glasses on as the sky over Amityville turned the purplish pink of a wound for miles out toward Brooklyn, Queens and the city.

One evening in early July I looked in my rearview mirror and saw a man in a red VW, waving. I swerved, thinking it was Sam, maybe Steve, and then realized that the car was a Pinto and that the man was Jason Donohue. Trying to stay in lane, I spread a piece of newspaper out across my lap. Checking twice to be sure no stretch mark showed, I waved back at Jason and pulled over.

"Hey," Jason said, glancing down at the paper, "heard you had mono." I rolled my eyes and leaned down to reach a page that had fallen. "So," he said when I did not elaborate, "heard you and Bono called it quits." I nodded and sighed, and Jason, not risking silence, began to talk: about his semester, his summer office job, about how freaking hard it was to find one interesting person or thing in Massapequa. I realized that I hadn't actually talked to Jason in years. And now, given the chance, I had nothing to say. But Jason spoke. "You can't even freaking get laid" is what he said. Winking, he added, "Let's get together if you have time," and walked back to his car.

Within five minutes of this encounter, I had temporarily forgotten my scars, the way my father looked at me and squinted, Steve, the Son of Sam, and whether or not, like Superman and Clark Kent, you'd ever see the two together in one room. I thought of Jason, who had winked. I tried to remind myself of sex.

At the library, skipping ahead to the *J* section, I checked out *Fear of Flying* by Erica Jong.

At work I stared with envy at Miriam's niece, a pale blonde named Claire who by coincidence went to Calverton and for now sat, rubbing her perfect thighs together, one desk to my left.

At 5:13, when Claire would shake me, saying, "Girl, wake up, it's time to split," I'd drive to see Darren Shapiro, now a gay artist, who enjoyed nothing more than to talk about sex —about masturbating into carved vegetables, about how he'd once woken up naked on the highway divider by Jones Beach, believing himself to be a reincarnation of Mark Rothko. I'd smile, usually, or say, "I can relate," then walk as quickly as I could down to Caro's, hoping she'd say something more ordinary, something perhaps to do with Jason.

Caro, most nights, sat flipping through magazines, occasionally asking things like, "Do you think the Bee Gees are gay?" One evening I did not answer. Instead, poking at a stretch mark above my knee, I asked her if she thought that Jason might someday come to like me. Caro looked at my leg, briefly at my face, then again at the area of flesh I'd quickly covered. Slowly she closed her mouth and then her most recent issue of *People*. "God," she said, "uh, I don't know. I mean, we'll have to see for you, okay?"

Jason called on Saturday to invite me, "last minute," to a company "bowling fest" that night at six. "Sure," I said, feeling around for my pulse, "sounds okay." Hanging up the phone, placing one hand to my heart, I added, "Shit."

My mother, who'd been listening, said, "No, it sounds like fun. Now do you know what you'll want to wear?"

"Mother, please," I said, "it's not *that* big a deal," and ran up the stairs three at a time to decide—foraging through closets and drawers, stomping through discarded piles of tops and skirts and settling at last for an old sundress of Gwyn's my mother had left on the door handle.

I emerged with it on hours later to find that it was barely two o'clock. My mother, it seemed, had managed to get everyone out so I'd have "breathing room." Sighing, I picked up a book and sat outside. Two minutes later the phone rang. I ran back in, but the person hung up as I answered. I walked outside and it rang again—with no one there. This happened three times. When it happened a fourth, I picked up without saying a word. I heard breathing. Then a voice like an exasperated math teacher's asked, "Elizabeth Israel?"

I said yes, and the woman explained that she was calling from the state of Connecticut and that she was required by law to ask me certain questions. Before I could say, "About what?" she started asking: "Number one, Miss Israel, can you tell me exactly why you chose to surrender your child to an adoptive couple?"

"What do you mean, 'surrender' it?" I asked.

"Miss Israel," she snapped, "let's not waste yours and my time: You had a baby. You surrendered it to an adoptive couple, is that correct?"

I wanted to say, "No shit, Sherlock," but sounding prim as Miriam Snee, said, "That's right."

"Well, then, Miss Israel, let me ask again—what specifically were your reasons for surrendering the child? Please be as specific as possible."

I was getting annoyed. I said, "I didn't see any other way."

Seeming just as annoyed, she asked, "Can't you please be more specific?"

"What else do you want to know?" I said. "I couldn't keep it. It was a mistake."

"Well, dear," she said, laughing quietly. "We're talking about a pretty serious mistake here, aren't we?"

I was going to give the Son of Sam this woman's address. Then she said, "Look, I know it's been rough on you. And I want you to understand that I'm not in any way judgmental. It's just my job to check up on things." She asked that I alert her as soon as possible to any problems and hung up, without giving me her number.

Walking across the lawn four hours later, I was still shaking. Jason noticed and handed me his jacket. By the time we'd reached the bowling alley I was sweating. Jason lifted the hair from my neck. He took my hand. I turned to face him. He said, "It's gonna be the anniversary of Sam's first killing—July 29. He's supposed to come to the South Shore. You better keep your freaking hair up." I opened my mouth and started crying. Jason let go of the hair and kissed my forehead. He kissed my cheek and then my lips, lightly, as he had that famous summer we were twelve. We sat there a while, songs from *Saturday Night Fever* on the radio, the hollow, cracking sounds of bowling behind us. At last I said, "Jason, I can't have sex with you." Jason turned up the radio and shrugged. "Okay," he said, "at least for now."

Son of Sam had promised to make his anniversary, July 29, a special day. Rumor had it that he planned to spell out his name—S A M—across the island, killing one or two girls at every point. And he had no intention on this, his anniversary, of sticking to girls in cars or to specific hair lengths or colors.

On July 28, in the office parking lot, I stopped to watch a stock boy tear up boxes by a dumpster. I had just finished *Fear of Flying* and was, for the moment, Isadora Wing, a cool erotic woman who did not fear the Son of Sam. I had gotten as far as mentally unzippering the boy's fly when a voice behind me said, "I have something for you."

I turned to find Steve, who had a sunburn. He was holding a paper bag.

"What is it?" I asked.

"It's for you," he said, "I got it in New Jersey."

Looking around, I said, "Steve. It's nice of you, but I'm going back to school. I'm leaving and you really shouldn't be buying me things anyway."

"Just look inside and see what it is. C'mon, Israel, it's a present. I can give you a present if I want."

I stuck my hand in and pulled out a pile of purple material.

Arranging it, I saw that it was a shirt, Indian-style and gauzy, with light purple pockets and paisley trim down the sides and sleeves.

"It's nice," I said.

Steve smiled. "It's for you."

"I appreciate it," I said, glancing at the stock boy, "but I don't think I can take it. Steve, you just cannot give me presents." I handed it back. The smile dropped from his face the way worn magnets fell from our refrigerator.

"Hey," he said, placing one finger beneath my chin, "I can give you anything I want, okay? We've been through some heavy shit. So you just can't push me off. You won't get away with it."

"Steve," I said, "it's just that you shouldn't be buying me presents," but Steve was walking away.

"Don't think I don't know what you're doing with Donohue," he said, slapping the hood of his car. "I got eyes."

He started the engine, a hand landed on my shoulder, and I jumped. It was Claire Snee, in tight designer jeans. "That's not the famous Jason, is it?" she asked, watching Steve leave tire tracks outside the Jewish cemetery. I shook my head and Claire said, "Good. Because I'd watch out for that guy if I were you."

I felt around in my purse for the codeine chip I'd found earlier. Swallowing it, I said, "Oh, he's just upset," and drove home, my head aligned with the dashboard, to call Jason, who picked me up and drove me several times around the Shores.

After one hour of this I began to wonder why, exactly, he was doing it—driving around with me, taking me bowling and then home again at 8:00 P.M. when I flipped out. I was about to ask but noticed that we were coasting down the hill by the canal. The car stopped just feet from the site of the sunken barge. "What are you doing?" I asked. "We shouldn't be parked in a car."

Jason placed a hand on my knee. "I'll move it," he said, "if you'll tell me why you won't sleep with me."

"Jason, please," I begged.

"It can just be for a minute," he offered. "Forget whatever the fuck happened. You can keep your shirt on."

A car turned onto the hill behind us. "All right," I muttered as the headlights grew larger, "but move, come on, and just not tonight, okay?" Jason rubbed my shoulder, put the car in drive and said, "Then it's a date."

At home I heard that Sam, as promised, had shot a non-brunette—a blond Brooklyn girl named Stacy. I barely slept that night and in the morning grabbed the paper from Gwyn to see the photos. There was a lump by Stacy's eyebrow the size of a yo-yo. Her mouth seemed to float on her face, a woozy pink amoeba beneath the nose. I handed the paper back to Gwyn and ran to call Steve's just to see if he was there. His mother answered, kept me on half an hour and then said, my heart seeming to sink with each word, "He went off in a huff somewhere—last night. I haven't seen him."

I went to bed after calling Steve's and stayed there one week, claiming cramps. I lay awake listening to my father slam down the phone at 3:00 A.M., waiting for Steve to break in with a gun. But by the end of the week my fears were less specific. It was possible, I conceded, that Steve was not the Son of Sam. The truth might have been that Steve was upset, afraid of losing me, and that I was just afraid—of everyone, of what people, like my father, might say to remind me, or not say, which the secretarial girls in the mall and the 3:00

A.M. caller had proved was worse. But it was August 8. Although I tried not to think about it, in two short weeks I'd leave for school. In twenty-four hours I'd be on my date with Jason. I could not reasonably spend the rest of my life running home if someone whispered, or running out if the phone rang late at night. And then there was my date.

I got up the next morning and walked to the mirror to see if perhaps a miracle had occurred in the night. I lifted my "Beatlemania—relive it at the Winter Garden" T-shirt and found that it had not. You'll just have to hide it, I thought, letting go of the shirt. And so I walked, in search of tools, into the bathroom.

Reviewing the contents of the medicine chest, I picked out liquid foundation, adhesive tape and gauze. Back in the room I applied the makeup base and placed the tape over it, wrapping it around my waist several times so I looked injured. But when I moved, the tape gapped, I had to put more tape on the tape, and it became hard to lift my arms. I unraveled it, put a tube top on first, but the problem of movement remained. What I had to do, I said as I kneaded the skin, was to fold the blubber over, tucking it in so that it stayed in place. What I needed was something more permanent than tape.

I trotted down to my father's workroom and looked around. I passed over tape and staples. I examined rubber bands and paper clips. My eyes stopped on Krazy Glue. I picked up the tube and rolled it in the palm of my hand. Stuffing it into my pocket, I ran back upstairs.

The glue was cold on my flesh so I worked quickly, folding the flab to the center and pressing. It *worked*, as they said in commercials, and so easy too! Pleased, I looked at it from all sides and reached for the tube to apply coat two. But suddenly my skin was on fire. Panting, I grabbed at the folded flesh. I ran a nail down the crease. I almost called for my mother but instead just pulled and tugged until at last the skin curled open, blood rushing in tiny red dots to the surface. I stood there stunned by what I had done. Then I dressed the wound, put some tape on the tape and rode my bike to Jason's, one hand at my ear in case of Sam, Steve or whomever.

Jason, as I arrived, put Eric Clapton on the stereo. He mixed two rum-and-Cokes, pointed to the couch and whispered, "There." I took my drink and sat, trying to ignore the way he nearly pulled the buttons off my blouse. On the last button I stood up. "Look," I said, "I got some serious sun poisoning on my stomach, so, um, try to be careful, okay?" Jason shrugged. "Whatever," he said, "you can just take off your pants if you want." After considerable discussion I did, and Jason, removing his own, proceeded to straddle me. I tried to concentrate. But what I pictured was the lacy-top girl as she'd sat the day I'd gone for my IUD, breast-feeding pudgy twins. As Jason pressed inside me I saw Stacy, the dead girl, her eye the colors of half-cooked meat, her mouth mushy as a piece of damaged fruit. I started to scream, louder than I had that day in the car with my mother, or ever. I screamed, "Don't touch me." Jason stopped moving his hips and looked down. Some explanation, I knew, was in order.

Thinking a minute, I said, "I had a bad abortion."

Jason's penis limped out onto my leg in response. "It's cool," he said, rolling off me. He reached for a cigarette. When the doorbell rang seconds later he leapt up, looking relieved. From the bathroom, where I'd made the mistake of cleaning my wound with rubbing alcohol, I peeked out to see Caro and Rainbo, who wore a necklace made of copper bells. I heard Jason say, "Actually we were gettin' kind of bored— glad you two stopped by," and then the familiar sound of girls whispering. But through the bells I could not make out what they were saying.

Son of Sam was captured that night at his apartment house in Yonkers. I nearly cried when I heard the news and ran downstairs at dawn to see the paper. Beneath the *Newsday* banner David Berkowitz was being led away in handcuffs. He looked, I thought, like fake-Cousin Donnie on Benzedrine.

The night before I went back to school I sat in the kitchen drinking coffee with my sisters. When my sisters went to bed I sat alone considering, as if for the first time, that I'd be going back—with Claire in several hours—to Calverton State College. I tried to remind myself why. I reviewed the importance of finishing what one had begun; I recalled how in May I'd been far too nervous and upset to plan for much else. I said to myself, At least you'll know where the library is if you want to hide—but a noise in the yard made me stop. I walked cautiously to the side door, where, framed in the top square of screen, I saw Steve.

"What do you want?" I asked, opening the door half an inch.

"You're makin' a fool out of me."

"Steve," I said, stepping outside. "What the fuck are you talking about? Can't you leave me alone even on my last night?"

"You've been fooling around with Donohue. He's one of my buddies. Don't think I don't know."

"It's a free country, Steve."

"Just remember what I know, my dear."

"Don't you dare threaten me after all you put me through—"

Steve grabbed my wrist. "You listen, sweetie," he hissed. "You put yourself goddamned through it, and you dragged me down with you. Now we're in it together, and don't you fucking forget it."

"Lower your voice, damn you. I am not your property."

"You remember one thing," he said, backing out toward the gate. "You just remember that I'm gonna keep my eye on you. You remember that, you fucking bitch."

I slammed the door as hard as I could and turned to find my father, in his bathrobe. I could tell that this was going to be a speech. Hoping to sound casual, I said, "Hi."

"Hello," he said as he moved toward me. "Just checking in, wanted to see how you were doing. I supposed you're all packed."

"Yeah, all ready," I said, watching the floor tile.

"Look, Bets," he said, "you've been avoiding me all summer. I try to talk to you or to sit next to you, and you run off. Now, it's clear that you haven't wanted to discuss what happened. You've had to keep to yourself. I understand that. But can't I please have just a moment of your time? Just a minute, I promise."

With my heart pounding, I followed him into the living room. He sat down and folded his hands as if to pray. "Please, sit," he said. I obeyed and folded my hands to match his.

My father sighed, preparing to speak. I stood and said, "I know that you want to talk about it, but I don't want to talk about it—not now and maybe never. I'm sorry, but you can't hold me back with this. I'm leaving, and you'll just have to accept that." I kissed him, kissed my mother at the top of the stairs and closed my door.

My mother was back at 6:00 A.M. with coffee. I drank it in the beanbag chair, where I'd sat and gotten stuck sometime near midnight. I tried to think of ways to make myself move. But the fear I'd felt at twelve had, by six, divided and spread so that it lay like a steel sheet across my chest: I did not dare think one second about the past; I could not, as the sky grew lighter, quite picture the future. I would just have to stay carefully where I was—drinking my coffee in small sips;

dressing for a long drive; taking only one speck of experience at a time. Observing the ratty pink shag carpet, then, wondering if it would at last be gone when I returned, I carried the suitcase, packed one night in June, back downstairs, each step squeaking once behind me as I went.

T E N

Late in the day, August 28, 1977, I stood, dropping things, at the center of campus. Claire Snee, whom I'd already named my new best friend, picked up a plant and handed it to me. "Well," she said, tossing one thin duffel over a bony shoulder, "take care, I guess," and then she walked off.

Struggling with my suitcase, three plants and the beanbag chair, I made my way to the new dorm. The two other rooms in the suite hallway were sealed, tight as motel glasses still in plastic. Inside my own I found two stripped beds and sets of matching dressers and desks. Standing there, objects falling to the floor, I thought of an essay I'd read for Humanities A called "Classical Interpretations of Hell." I closed the door, said, "Forget it, unpack," and for an hour moved one pair of jeans from bed to chair. Giving that up, I hung the Mont-St.-Michel painting above the phone. I cried for a while, then lay down on the bed by the window. When I woke up it was dark, and a girl somewhere with a guitar was singing the Joni Mitchell song about the baby the mother cannot keep—". . . Little Green, have a happy ending . . ."—which I interpreted as karma or fate, and then it stopped. I got up to see where the voice had come from, but the hall was still sani-sealed, all rooms completely silent.

When I returned from registration the next day, my new roommate was sucking on an asthma inhaler, mumbling "uh-huh" into the phone. Hanging up, she announced that her name was Roberta, that she was a music therapy major, but that she had, really, no time to talk right now. She picked up the phone again, and I raced out to buy her a flower, a symbol of the friendship we would share. But Roberta was gone when I returned.

Blowing out an exaggerated breath, I put the flower, a daisy, on Roberta's bed and sat on mine to flip through a book called *Minds or Bodies*. I felt light-headed as I read, my skin sensitive to touch as if I had fever. The girl with the folky voice sang, "I could drink a case of you," and it occurred to me that I had not eaten in days. I sat pretending to read for a while, then picked up the phone and dialed my old number. Suzi Butkes answered. "Well, well," she said, "we didn't think we'd be hearing from you again." After a pause she added, "But sure, I don't see why we can't have lunch."

On line at Erie Dining Hall, Big Suzi ran her eyes with Hoover precision over my waist region. "Let's see," she said, focusing for the first time on my face, "Christina, your former roommate, works in a bank at home. But I guess you guys . . . well. Sarie is still running the birth-control clinic, same as last year, but I guess you knew that, right?"

I had not known that. All I remembered of Sarie was the way she'd gripped my shoulders at the Christmas party and said, "Let's let Betsy play Santa, whaddya say, girls?" as if I were Tiny Tim, the little lame one. "What about Laroo?" I asked.

"Oh, Roo's still around."

"Great," I said, "I'll call her."

Suzi sucked in her breath and said, "I'd wait on that."

I changed the subject. "So," I asked, "have you tried the bulgur?"

As I was about to take my first bite of bulgur, Suzi waved to a friend of Christina's, Anette Serini, who had lived in the suite next to ours. Anette sat down, glanced at Suzi, then fixed her eyes on my forehead. "So, Betty," she announced, "*you've* lost weight."

Suzi kicked her so hard the table shook. I dropped my fork and stood up. "Come on, girl," said Suzi, "finish your bulgur," but I was moving away and then running, and did not stop until I threw open my door to see the daisy, one petal missing, lying limply on my bed. Roberta was sitting on hers, surrounded by three other girls and a wine bottle.

"Uh, look," she said as I skimmed *Minds or Bodies,* "I really don't want you making my bed, okay?"

"I'm sorry," I said. "You just looked so busy and I'm not as busy yet, that's all."

"Well, just don't, okay?"

One of the girls giggled. "Fine," I said, "I won't."

I picked up *Minds or Bodies* and walked out past the folky voice, down to the creek where in a previous life I had picked grapes with Dhani. I sat on a rock and cried for half an hour, then resolved not to cry for at least two additional days—until September 1. Roberta was gone again when I got in, but there were two notes. One, with an address, said, *Donny called—got your number from operator and invites you Sat.* The other, in large and loopy writing, said, *Who are you? You look interesting, a little manic. Sally Slit, your nabe.*

Classes began September 2 and I tried to stay out of my room, away from Roberta, for as many hours as possible. I joined the student newspaper as a features reporter. I signed on for six additional classes in unlikely subjects such as Literature of Sixteenth-Century Spain and Death, Dying, and Decision: The Ethics of Suicide. I hoped to see Dhani, Sally Slit, the girl who sang, or Claire, who lived, like Dhani, somewhere off-campus, but I saw no one. Roberta, whom I saw most often lying with a wet towel over her face, spoke only once that first week.

She said, "I will be moving off-campus. Nothing personal, but I cannot breathe in this environment."

I had a quick vision of myself alone, of an entire semester spent asking people at Erie if I could please join them as girls kicked one another or giggled. I lay down on my bed and said, "Don't worry, I understand," and was still lying there at midnight when the phone rang. Roberta interrupted her packing to pick it up.

"It's an obscene phone call," she whispered. She listened another minute, then looked at me. "Oh, my God," she said, "it's for you."

I struggled up to grab the phone, but the caller had gone. Roberta sneezed. "He sounded like a maniac," she said. "Great," I replied, gathering my blankets. Roberta shrugged and went back to her packing. I walked to the living room, said, Two days have passed, and started crying. One hour later I heard a noise, the sound of a man's heavy boots in the stairwell, and stopped. I thought of rape, of knifings out in the quad. Get up, I said to myself, run, but I was too depressed, too tired, and just sat there as a chubby girl with a dented guitar, a frizzy shag three shades of brown and blond and rhinestone-studded glasses curling up like Gwyn's fourth-grade pair dropped down into a chair. She said, "Fuck."

Pulling a worn Frye boot from beneath heavily patched jeans, she croaked, "So how come you didn't write back, man?"

It was Janis Joplin, I thought, fresh out of good women and in need of Jack Daniel's. Then I remembered. "Oh," I said, untangling my blankets, "you're Sally Slit."

Janis roared. "Slit? Well, I suppose there are those who would agree. I meant 'Sliv'—as in Slivowitz, as in Jap manquée, as in 'Miss Silverware, is that a Jewish name?' Do you have any cigarettes? This fucking guy is ripping my deposit off from where I lived when I split home last summer. Bastard fucking asshole. He also took my cigarettes and Charlie Blue, my oldest fucking guitar in the world. Now I'm stuck in this hole with these primpy cunts in the lockets and sweaters. They iron their fucking blue jeans."

I could not think of one thing to say. Sally put her foot up on the arm of my chair and said, "Hey. You look like either you shoot speed into your thigh or you got wheels on your Frye boots. And now I finally meet you and you just veg." She picked up her guitar and, imitating Joe Cocker, sang, "Yooou are a veg-table to me," then laughed and stopped. "Just kidding," she said, squinting. "So, like, what's your problem?"

Staring out into the quad, the sidewalks crisscrossed like the lines on my body, I considered telling her just to see how it would sound. Instead, thinking back to Jason's, I said, "I had an abortion."

Sally found a cigarette in her sock. "Big fucking deal," she said, lighting it. "I've had three. So fucking what."

"But it left scars," I told her, slightly excited. "It left bad scars."

Sally stood and pulled off her shirt, revealing breasts the shape and size of mature eggplants. "You see this?" she said, pointing to strips of white on her upper arms, "and this? These are burns, man—fucking scars. We all got fuckin' scars. To be a woman is to be scarred."

I asked, "Were you in a fire? Were you seriously burned?"

"No," Sally said, yawning, "I work the oven at fucking Pizza Hut in my fascist hometown of White Plains."

I told her that my roommate was moving out and Sally explained how I could conspire to keep the room to myself. I told her that I thought I should have a roommate because I was just coming back and Sally told me to grow up. "You're a woman," she said, leaning over to pick up her shirt. "So you've had some shit come down. But you're a woman and that's just what it is." Sally stood, hoisted her guitar and lumbered out half naked.

Sitting there alone, I could not imagine enough time ever passing so that I could walk from a room half undressed. I could not at that point imagine keeping up my end of a conversation. Chewing the skin around one fingernail, I waited for morning.

The following weekend I walked down to Dhani's, to what looked like a miner's home in a PBS special about Appalachia. There was a sort of chicken coop on the front lawn and black tape over cracks in the windows. The smell of sandalwood wafted out onto the porch. From the stereo came the kind of tone music in which the same note is played, with slight variations, over a chorus singing the one note. "Dhani," I called, slightly dizzy. "Hello?"

Dhani was sitting in the kitchen wearing one of the blue-and-white shawls around his shoulders. Without looking up, he asked if I had read the book he'd given me at Christmas, *The Prophet*. I did not remember any book. I said, "I skimmed it."

"Then, my friend," he said, looking down into his teacup, "you did not read it."

I reminded him that I'd been sick; it had been hard to concentrate.

Dhani turned to face me. He said, "You were not really sick."

My heart skipped a beat. I said, "What do you mean? I had mono. It was a drag."

Dhani said, as if speaking to someone across the room, "Watch the candle." I watched it. Dhani cleared his throat. "See the way it was once an entire work of wax?" he asked, "an object of value someone molded, hardened into a specific form? Notice then that it burned. Your illness," he concluded with eyes closed, "was like this candle. A weakening under the pressure of those things that formed you."

Dhani, it turned out, had been on a juice fast six days. He

was losing strength and suggested that we lie down to rest on the floor. Lying there, the stereo skipping on one tone so that it sounded like a hiccup, he continued to relate his view of my intellect: how I engaged in little more than continuous obfuscation; how my very "being" was a mere repository for petty untruths.

"Dhani," I said, adding to the litany, "I got pregnant."

About half an hour later Dhani said, "Why tell me this?"

"Because maybe it's you who got me pregnant," I blurted, "and then I had to have a very bad abortion and I got a lot of stretch marks. Here, look." I pulled up my shirt.

I had no idea why I'd said this, except that pretending it was anyone other than Steve had a certain appeal. But I wished I hadn't: My heart beat so violently I was afraid it might stop. It occurred to me for a minute that Dhani's had stopped already, that I'd caused it and lay now with a corpse. Climbing over him, tucking in my shirt, I said, "Thank you for inviting me over," and ran back to campus, one hand on the skin pouch, convinced that a normal conversation was beyond me.

At home Sally Sliv was waiting up. Standing at the center of my room, she lowered her jeans, removed a tampon and tossed it into the trash as casually as if she'd taken a cigarette from her pocket, then put it out. Some girls from next door came in later on with a hash pipe and two black guys followed with hash. Lying on the beds now pushed together, I wrote, *perhaps there are connections,* and fell asleep peacefully when everyone had gone. But at 3:00 A.M. the phone rang.

It sounded at first like a low rumble over static, but I gradually made out the voice of Steve. He used the word "slut." He said something about a gun and hung up. Leaning against the wall, I slid down all the way to the floor. In the morning I stood and walked to Sally's room, where she was asleep with the black men. I tried to think of someone else to

GROWN·UP FAST • 213

call, could not, and went by myself to breakfast, although I wasn't hungry. I walked for several hours around campus, then went home to find Sally still asleep with the men and the phone in my room ringing. No one was there when I answered.

By late September Steve's calls had become as much a part of my life as rewriting student newspaper articles deemed "overly imaginative." I would pick up, day or night, and Steve, in the manner of Norman Bates narrating a porn film, would explain how he planned to attack me with either a gun or "my fuckin' cock," because I was a "fuckin' slut" who had betrayed him. I wanted each time to hang up, to call a cop or just scream. But like a character glued to dirt in a dream, I'd stand there silent.

I had no history of action against Steve—I'd ignored various threats in the past by going home to my room or getting high. Now that I could, of course, call the police, I wanted no connection to him at all, and certainly not the kind involving cops. I'd just stand against the wall letting him talk. And, although it surprised me, as weeks went by I started listening. The more I heard them, the more Steve's diatribes seemed to form some disturbing piece of evidence—that despite Sam's capture, I was still doomed; that despite my new life, I would not escape the old one. *Any fate is possible,* I wrote once as he shouted, *that much I now know.* And so I stood there.

One night, however, Steve called me a Jew and then a cunt. I hung up. When the phone rang minutes later, I picked it up, screaming, "Leave me alone, you fucking asshole!"

My mother, at the other end, shouted, "What?"

"Oh, nothing," I said, forcing a laugh, "I was just kidding

around with my new close girlfriends," and continued to laugh as my father, picking up the extension, asked, "How are you, babe? How are you feeling? Handling things okay?"

My father spoke about Spain during the 1500s. My mother said she'd seen Caro. I told them, in exchange, about my feature stories and my classes, about how I'd dropped a few because ten was too many. They asked if there was anything else and if I'd heard from Massapequans. I pictured Steve rasping into the phone. I pictured my father punching the table so hard Gwyn dropped her fork, the vibrations working their way out, causing Sashi to cry and my mother to say, "Honey, please." I had caused enough trouble. "Just Caro," I said, "I gotta go."

By mid-October it had become clear that Dhani was through with me. I had called him. I had stood outside a window with tape on it and yelled. But he ignored me, devoting himself to a girl who painted a fluorescent red dot slightly off-center on her forehead. I followed them to campus films, to the student Rat, through the Humanities hall, and one day down the main street that led to his house. Halfway there, Dhani stopped and walked back to meet me.

"What a coincidence," I said.

"Please," he replied, "you must put a stop to this. Now, I think it was very progressive of you to have been so intimate with a Palestinian such as myself, but it's time to move on."

I said, "A Palestinian?"

Dhani gripped my shoulders. "You must stop following us," he said. "You are upsetting Bernadette."

He walked off and I stood there watching him, genuinely afraid that I would never understand anything about anything again: One year your mother is hemming your prom dress;

the next, there's a gash like a canyon through your life. Steve
is a psycho; Dhani, it turns out, is an Arab. I looked up. It
was snowing.

Other men soon appeared. Some left poems on my door and
some stood beneath my window playing "Teach Your Children" on guitars until I'd call the front desk to make them
stop. My favorite one—the one least like Steve and most like
Dhani, only American—ran the counter downtown at Taco
Heaven.

He was, I'd immediately sensed, a "meaningful leftover"—
a fully bearded member of the ten-years-too-late set I'd ob-
served on the Thanksgiving bus. His name was Glenn Boxer,
which he'd changed from Weisblatt after his favorite Simon
and Garfunkel song. Like Dhani, he would often stare at a
person intently, then, without warning, close his eyes to
chant. In explanation he'd say, "I am only a raggedy man out
peacefully in the world." Sally translated: "He's from fucking
asshole White Plains. He went to Ethical Culture." One
night Glenn, whoever he was, made me a burrito and said,
"Tell me a story." I told him that a disturbed man with white
hair called me in the night. The next day Glenn Boxer appeared at my door with his life's possessions. He had come, he
said, to answer my phone.

We lived in my room along with Sally—who couldn't get
the two black guys to leave hers "without seeming hung-up
and racist"—Glenn's 400 records, thirty homemade bongs,
his red Lava lamp and a tree trunk he'd saved since childhood.
When the sun went down we'd plug in the Lava, sit on the
beds and wait for Steve to call. Glenn had prepared a coun-
terattack. "Hey, man," he'd counsel, "you should work
through this shit." Sally, handing me my down coat, would

say, "Ignore that bastard asshole fascist pig," and out we'd walk to scrape the snow off Glenn's BMW so we could drive to the all-night pancake place, where we'd sit until dawn.

Glenn had understood when I'd explained that I could not, for various reasons, engage in sex. Like many meaningful leftovers, he claimed to have had his own "heavy shit come down"—even if, in the same way they all claimed to be musicians, the specifics remained vague. One November day, though, he said, "You must try to loosen up." I backed away, asking, "How exactly do you mean?" Glenn, walking toward me, said, "Calm yourself, lady. I am not pressing you for sex, I merely copped some superlative LSD." Backed up in a corner, I said, "No way." Glenn, who stood over me, chanted, "If you have not seen the snow when high, then you have not done your LSD." Sally burst in, threw a pillow at me and said, "Fucking come on. It'll be fun."

We dropped acid that Friday with ten others, all of whom, at Glenn's instigation, wanted to walk around campus falling backward into snowdrifts. I managed to talk them out of this by saying, "Why don't we first walk around the dorm?" Sally said, "Yeah, we'll judge by the doors how creative our straight asshole neighbors are." And so we formed a parade, stopping at doors with posters of kittens and doors with erasable message pads that said "We R Not Here." Sally would shout, "Pathetic," and we'd move on.

The two winning doors were covered with newspaper—the first a concrete poem, items about bombs glued together in the shape of a missile; the second, a collage of articles chronicling odd instances of baby abuse. I pretended with the others that I found this clever and read on: There was Frank, the baby masher from Idaho; Mike from southern California, who'd put a baby in the microwave; the Georgia babysitter who'd locked one in the trunk of her car. The group walked on, and I, noticing the edges of the last tiny item start to

GROWN·UP FAST · 217

ripple, read about the corrupt baby seller, the lawyer who was said to have used young white girls to get their babies, which he sold at huge profit on the black market. He was from New York City. He was thirty-eight. His name was Lawrence Stein. My jaw dropped like a loose zipper. The door opened. I put my hand on the hinge to steady myself, just as the guy who'd opened it to scream "Shut the fuck up" slammed it closed. I was so stunned I did not immediately feel the pain. Seconds later I moaned, "Oh, my God," and fell to the ground.

They stood over me. Glenn said, "Hey, lady. Why so blue?"

For days I tried to figure out what this meant without being forced to call my parents to ask. This they could not handle. In truth, I did not want to know all that badly myself. I was afraid I'd have to testify at his trial, although I hadn't known what he was going to do. And what exactly had he done? Did it mean the people on the mimeographed sheet weren't the people in the parking lot? Was the social-work bitch only Mrs. Stein in disguise? I thought of her husband and his obsession with that contract clause—a basic concern, I'd thought, with resolving all sticky points early on. But now I guessed that he'd been trying to assess my state of mind; by nagging me about the future he'd hoped to gauge whether or not I might reappear at some point to make trouble. I remembered how he'd asked, "You're sure, now?" after I'd chosen to leave the files open. I wondered if closed files guaranteed neater, more lucrative sales. I picked up the phone and listened to Steve, who called three times a day just to sob.

One night during finals, Glenn shrieked, "Enough," ripped the phone from the wall and placed it alongside me on the bed. "This, lady," he said, "is my Chanukah gift to you."

In celebration we had sex, partially clothed, in the beanbag chair. Sally came in the next morning to say that the black men had left. Claire Snee stopped by later on to say hello; it turned out that she lived in the same house as Roberta, my first and short-lived roommate. "Good, you deserve each other," I said as I closed the door on her face. The semester, I told myself, was almost over. I'd declared a double major, in English and French; I'd been elected to the student newspaper board. Nothing had been said about Mr. Stein.

The day we were scheduled to drive home, there was a lot of mail: my parents' annual hand-printed card; a card from Gwyn; one from Caro and, stuck high in the slot, a large pink envelope addressed in a handwriting that gave me chills. I carried it with me into a nearby bathroom. Ripping it open, I found a large white card bordered in pink and blue silk roses. Raised gold script spelled out *Happy Mother's Day.* Through it all ran a thick black X. It was signed, *An old friend.*

I tore the card into small pieces, flushed them down the toilet and walked behind Glenn and Sally Sliv out to the car. It was snowing again, a thin, tickly snow that stuck to the eyelashes. My two friends were stuffing it down each other's pants. Glenn asked what had been in the envelope. I coughed and said, "Oh, just a card." They agreed it was weird that a girl named Israel got Christmas cards.

"But she's the Madonna," Glenn said, kissing my head. "The Virgin Betsy."

Sally hit him and said, "You sexist asshole. It's 1977. Grow the fuck up," and I took a hit off a joint from some kid who'd fallen in step behind Glenn. I passed it to Sally and turned my face up into falling snow, my eyes wide as I could get them. I had decided to see how long I could go without blinking.

E L E V E N

The last time I saw Steven Bono
was on New Year's 1978, at 4:25 A.M. I was asleep at the
time in my room. It occurred to me as I lay there that the
dog, who'd been asleep too, was now howling. I was about to

see why when I heard a noise at the window—the sound of glass shattering—and sat up as the blind bulged out like a cyst.

"Who is it?" I gasped. The blind flew up in response. Steve, heavier than the last time I'd seen him, sat perched on the ledge like a huge stuffed bat, brushing glass out of his crotch and belching.

At first I said nothing. Then, swallowing several times, I asked, "What do you want?"

Steve thought about it. Looking past me toward the closet he said, "Why won't you talk to me?"

I couldn't believe that this was what he had come to ask. I couldn't believe that I was standing on my bed in a Calverton T-shirt, thinking of what to say in response. My parents' bed creaked. I said, "Get the fuck out of here," but Steve just sat there, staring out at my closet. My parents came padding down the hall. I said, "Get out of here *now.*" The doorknob turned, and Steve seemed to lean back and fall just as my father clutched my arm and yelled, "Who did this?"

I stammered a minute, then said, "It was Steve."

My father slapped the door frame and stomped out. My mother sighed, put her arm around me and walked me down to the kitchen, where Gwyn was already making tea, arranging mandel cake into a fan shape on one of Nanny Etta's plates. My father passed us on his way out the door, a felt hat on his head, a World War II rifle in his hand. But as the tea water boiled he came back in. Steve had gone.

Steve was arrested the next day, charged with criminal trespassing, then released and placed on probation. His mother called me to apologize in his behalf: "He's caused enough trouble for one lifetime. That's what I told him—and I think now he sees it." As she spoke, I pictured someone peeling a rusty Brillo pad from a sink. I hung up, went back to school two weeks early, told Glenn Boxer the real reason I did not want to have sex and, once he'd stopped crying in empathy, explained that I'd have to change the phone number, then move. During the remaining two years of college, while taking, on average, twenty-three credits per semester and spending an estimated sixty-five hours each week in the student newspaper office and at various jobs, I moved an additional ten times—with Glenn, the three boyfriends who followed him, with Sally Sliv and other friends.

At my request we never mentioned Steve in my family, or Mr. Stein, whose face I'd seen, one day in 1978, on the inside page of a *New York Post* my father had tried to keep hidden. Only Sashi asked me once, my first postcollege fall in New York, if I ever missed Caro or Val, or my old life. I was standing in my living room, stuffing page proofs into a black purse the size of a mail sack. Annoyed, I said, "No, they were part of the horrible past. I am too busy to think about them —or it—for one second."

She hesitated, then asked, "Well, do you ever think about the baby?"

I stopped stuffing and said, "What are you talking about?" the word "talk" sounding unexpectedly like "squawk."

"You remember," she said, speaking as if reading flash cards, "your baby."

Outside my window a pink sunset smooth as new subway tile was arching its way down St. Marks Place. Slinging the bag over one shoulder, I told her no. I tied the belt of a new black trench coat tightly around my waist. "No," I repeated, "the past, mercifully, is dead."

I liked the way this phrase sounded and said it quite often that year and in others, even if at times it was not entirely relevant to conversation.

In 1981 I decided to have plastic surgery. Although the stretch marks had faded to a veiny, shrimpish white, the skin pouch, even after four years, was still thick. Determined to be rid of it at last, I walked through the Upper East Side at lunch all that summer, lifting my shirt for wealthy surgeons. Tugging on the skin as if washing out a sweater, all agreed that I was sufficiently elastic to withstand the procedure. Each one said that I possessed the right attitude and that I was, at almost twenty-three, the right age. Only one, however, said it could be done for less than $5,000—the chief of plastic surgery at the Bellevue clinic.

He warned me that Bellevue was "no country club." Repeating, "You *do* understand this?" he advised me on insurance and told me that he was personally glad I'd be coming: "I've had three emergency micros this week—fingers, one hand—now I've got a nasty third-degree burn job and a pointless rhino. But you and me kid, we're going to have fun!" Nodding, I went back to work and told fellow editorial assistants and friends that I'd been hit by a car years before and left with scars. I told my parents not to worry—I'd be home, fully recovered, in a day or two. I checked myself into Bellevue.

I was wheeled first to a room with four beds, then led to another, brown-tiled room with four showers and no lights. A nurse handed me a bar of black soap. "You wash every inch of that body," she said, walking out. I nodded, took the soap and scrubbed in the dark, awaiting the inmate with the broom as had Linda Blair in women's prison movies on TV. I stood there for a while when I was through, then walked behind the nurse, who'd said, "Oh. I forgot about you," to some kind of supply closet. Dr. DeVito, the surgeon, appeared one hour later, said, "Been waiting long?" and then, "Okay, clothes off and up on the chair." Whistling, he drew a blue-dotted graph on my stomach, lifting the skin gingerly as he might have a testicle.

Back in my room that night I could not sleep. The woman

next to me with the double mastectomy could not sleep; the girl with the third-degree burns in the bed across could not stop crying. I lay there shaking and at dawn was wheeled to some other sort of closet, rolled over and shot with tranquilizers. As the cart I was on began to move, I realized that I had actually agreed to have surgery. I panicked and tried to sit up. A nurse barked, "Get a grip on her," which was, for me, like being on "This Is Your Life" and hearing the voice of your fifth-grade teacher. There was another shot, this one to the thigh, and I passed out.

I lay motionless the next day in Indian summer heat, watching a band of flies pad around on the lunch custard. There were visitors. My mother was able to say, "Well," before the color rushed from her cheeks. Sashi silently handed me *The Great Gatsby,* a book she was reading and thought I'd like. Gwyn called from college. "Now maybe it won't take you four hours to get dressed," she said as my father lit his pipe, against regulations, and asked, "So what was involved?"

"Oh, not much," I replied, though I could feel acutely how much was.

The pleated red drapes had been completely cut off and the remaining skin pulled down and sewn from hip to hip with more than 100 stitches. Dr. DeVito had crafted a belly button he described as "perky," though it was and would most likely stay numb. My family left me, reassured a thousand times that I felt better than I looked. For three days after, I lay saying the same thing to other visitors, fanning myself with *The Great Gatsby,* praying that it would look better than it felt.

On my last day at Bellevue, Dr. DeVito came in to unveil my new body. The stretch marks were still there, but with the skin so tight they seemed to blend, to form a pattern — the entire area like a swatch of plaid material smoothed but not ironed. "That's as good as it'll get," said my doctor, step-

224 • BETSY ISRAEL

ping back. I smiled and said, "It's beautiful." He winked at
me, said, "Okay, then," and walked out, stepping past a
blond middle-aged nurse on her way in. The nurse approached the bed and lifted my gown as if flipping back the
sheet on a dead person. "So," she said, smiling, "do you remember freaking out when we brought you in from OR?"

I said that I did not. Still holding the gown, she added,
"Well. This sure must have been one rough one. I take it, uh,
that you're not married."

Grabbing at my gown, I said, "That's none of your business."

"Touch-y," she said, folding her arms. "So, you can tell me
at least, is it a little girl or a little boy?"

It occurred to me that the nursing profession required certain distinct personality traits. I wondered if Rainbo Martin
or the secretarial girls had given it much thought. "Well?"
said the nurse.

As coolly as a nonchalant outside an abandoned storefront,
I smirked and said, "I can't remember."

In 1982 I ran into Darren Shapiro, the artist, outside a
Hawaiian restaurant on Seventh Avenue. Standing there in
my black trench coat, now minus one button, I told him that
I was a junior editor and that I was going to school at night
to get my Master's degree. Darren, who wore eye makeup and
tiny gold hoop earrings, said that he worked days as a commercial artist and nights, when not painting, as a male strip-
per. He had barely survived the holocaust of Tremor High, he
told me. He said that in nightmares Ken Puglia ate his intestines and that, to better escape the past, he had changed his
name to Charvé, after an African man he had met on a plane.
Turning onto Forty-second Street, we became friends.

On our free weekends we wandered the far West and Lower

East sides and occasionally, on a dare, walked all the way to Penn Station. Riding the South Shore local, we'd observe our hometown at a distance: Big Chief Lewis and his faithful bison cub, encircled now by electrified barbed wire; Mister Donut, the place girls had run to, home and out of breath from the city, all boarded up. And then, agreeing that we had ridiculously wasted an afternoon, we'd ride back.

In 1983 I came to notice—as one might gradually pick up on a trend in summer sandals—that I was surrounded by babies. Walking now and then through the Upper East Side, I'd fight my way through platoons of high-tech strollers. Walking into story meetings, I'd practically trip on the one or two kids writers would arrange, artfully, with toys on the floor.

Before then I had viewed babies from a distance. There were always the few around school, belonging to harried-looking girls who kept them strapped to their chests like large necklaces. Walking into the student Union, young mothers had always launched a chain of respectful nods. When they'd gotten up to leave, strangers had always offered rides, commenting, as the girls politely declined, on what "strong individuals" they were, "girls with real guts." Watching them struggle not to drop baby or books, I had felt less respect than swelling nausea, chills racing all around my body as if someone had rubbed tin foil on my nipple.

By the mid-1980s, however, there seemed to be no avoiding infants.

One night during the summer of 1984, an editor I knew named Arlette threw a party to introduce hers, as the invitation put it, "to *amis et famille*." The crowd at this gathering was the usual cross section of investment banker trainee, freelance writer, and artist working most recently in egg carton and wire. As I had at high school parties, I tried to trace exactly how I'd come to be at this one, holding a drink I did not want. But Arlette approached with the baby, named Danton, and began to shout into my forehead about what "an entirely extraordinary experience" his birth had been. Coming up from the rear was her husband to describe, in clinical detail, what the placenta had felt like as he held it. This reminded me of the colleague at my last job who had told me that he'd put his tongue to the placenta, "an act of first bonding," carrying on for so long that I had to have my assistant fake a call.

Arlette gave me Danton to hold "because you're so *single!*" then wafted off. I placed petit Danton on a nearby chair and walked into a bathroom, where I cut four thin lines of the coke I'd found tucked inside a boyfriend's sock that morning. Bypassing Danton, I retrieved my black trench coat, which had lost yet another button, and ran out to catch a cab.

Finally asleep some ten hours later, I found myself inside an eerie dream.

I was walking through the old Bar Harbour shopping center. The stores were boarded up, but the store signs— Gimbels, Kresge's, Lobel's, Grant's—were still blinking, the neon dripping out the tips of letters like heated Jell-O. About halfway down the concourse, I noticed a tiny person in black boots and a black hooded cape in the distance. It occurred to me that the person was Val, I thought I should say hello, and I walked toward her. But then the person started moving toward me, I couldn't see her face, and I stopped. I looked down at the cracked cement pavement. I looked down into the brick planter at my side, the kind that had been filled with pink azalea in summer. The only thing in it now was a white smile-face button embedded in dirt. I kneeled to pick it up, but the button was stuck. I began digging for it, then scratching, pulling at it so furiously my fingers bled. Stopping, I could hear myself breathe. I could hear my heart beat. Behind me I heard a noise. "Betsy," said a high giggly girl's voice, "turn around."

My mother, running into The Gnome, would often collect information about Marie-Ellen Val Scarparelli. She had, as of 1984, left the tall, mysterious Victor in favor of a man who had gained her attention by driving onto the sidewalk of the Shore East Diner one week before it burned. She'd gotten an apartment with this new man, then a house and then a boat, burrowing deeper into the center of Long Island—Copiague, Lindenhurst, Islip—and secretarial jobs, vanishing into the world of paneled dens and gray metal desks without a trace.

Caro Carroway was the only girl of the era who called, the first time in 1980, on the night John Lennon died. Beatle songs played in the street; someone outside in the hall said, "So, I guess there'll be some openings in the Dakota." Caro, out on Long Island, said, "So, let's have dinner. John would have wanted it that way." The people in the stairwell chuckled, then moved on. The song "Help" floated up from the street.

"I'm sorry," I told Caro. "I have a deadline on a piece. I have to go." She called again a few times. Once out of curiosity, in the fall of 1984, I said okay.

We got trapped in the rain that night and stepped quickly inside an old Italian place in the Village. In a thick accent I'd never noticed, Caro talked—about her college experiences, her job as a stewardess, about why it was great to still live home, and about how Boat, her ex-flame, had died after driving his car into a pole on the Wantagh State Parkway. Shocked, I thought sentimentally a moment about the late Boat Brody. What I pictured was a thick cock balanced on the tip of my nose and then a hand smashing my face. I said nothing. Caro, disturbed by this silence, pulled an envelope from her purse. "Oh, great," I said, a chill crawling up my spine like a cockroach, "pictures."

In a shot of Jason's wedding, Ken Puglia and Jim Scabb stood with arms locked around slightly slimmer versions of their mothers. Caro said, "You remember Debbie," and I looked closely at one girl and saw, encased in a double chin like a piecrust, the face of a secretary detective.

"Of course," I said, "I just didn't recognize her with her mouth closed." Caro looked at me, confused, then changed the picture.

There was Jason: tan, though it had been winter, both chunky arms around the bride—one of the girls, I recalled, so stoned in eighth-grade gym she could not cross to her left during a folk dance of the Balkans. Alongside them stood Denise "Rainbo" Martin, who, as Mary Martin, had become a born-again Christian; some others I did not know; and then Steve, his waist spread prematurely, his hairline receding, down on one knee in front of the crowd. He looked drunk. I said, "Let's get the check."

Walking up to Fourth Street, Caro asked if I'd ever heard again from Steve.

"God, no," I said. In truth, one night the year before, he'd actually called me.

I'd immediately threatened to call the police, a lawyer, the FBI. "There is a court order that says you cannot do this," I said through clenched teeth.

"I know that," said Steve. "I called you anyway."

"Look," I said, "I am an associate editor. Next month I am going to China."

Steve said that he was glad. There were, however, a few things he had to say, and he planned at this time to say them.

I paused a long time, then said, "What?"

Steve cleared his throat. "First, you gotta know that in all my life, there is just this one thing that I can never live with. And, it's like, even if everything is okay, there's always this thing that I hurt you, and even though we went through it together, you won't ever talk to me."

"Steve, please," I said. Steve interrupted.

"It just lays in my mind and won't leave. I feel like I did this terrible thing. But I'm twenty-six years old now. It's fucking Saturday night, and I'm in Babylon. I don't even know if I'm going out. I don't even know what job I'm gonna do this week."

I paused again, took a deep breath and said, "Okay, Steve. Let me say that I am sorry about your weekend. I am even more sorry about your career. But that is the extent of how sorry I am. Steve, you are not my friend. You are not even an acquaintance in my life. That you once were has to do more with circumstance, a very weird situation, than it does with how I felt. Now that's not to say I didn't care for you and sometimes have fun with you. But the point is, Steve, that we came from very different worlds, and even without this disaster we would very shortly, in 1976, have gone back to them. Forgive me, Steve, but your parents didn't even have bookshelves.

"And, Steve, you think we went through some experience together? You had an experience of your own and I had mine, and we emerged from them in very different ways. Now you listen—I *made* something from that bullshit drugged-out nightmare I used to call a life; you seem to have wallowed in it. And you know something, Steve? It's *your* fucking problem, not mine. It wasn't mine in 1977. It most certainly is not mine in 1983. Now I am very glad we had a chance to have this little talk, but I am tired—no, make that *sick to death*—of being haunted by you, harassed and threatened, and I'm not going to tolerate it one more second. There is nothing left to say, and I want you to hang up this phone and never bother me again or I *will* call the police."

"So what," Steve said, "you don't even wanna have dinner with me?"

Exasperated, I said goodbye, hung up, got an unlisted number and flew the next day to London to report a story. Darren-Charvé, who had moved to Paris and changed his name to Etienne, flew in to meet me.

Back out in the rain that night, Caro said, "Don't you wanna at least split a cab?" I looked at her and searched for something to say, for some explanation or summary of our friendship that would make sense. I realized as we stood there getting wet that there wasn't one. "I prefer to walk," I finally said, blew a kiss somewhere in the vicinity of her cheek, began to walk and then to run. I turned back once to look. Caro was still standing on the corner staring after me, her arms protectively hugging the purse that held the pictures.

Sometime in early 1985 I began to have trouble sleeping. If I happened to drift off, in a chair or on a couch, I'd wake up minutes later, unsure of where I was. I'd walk around my apartment, looking in closets and corners. In a notebook I'd write, *I am under great stress since I took the new job, and far worse since the promotion.* By July, when I could sleep at most two nights per week, I'd write, *I have a constant headache, due to reading in bad light, and cannot eat because of the disgusting heat and unbelievable stress, which is worse because of unrealistic deadlines.*

On the two rested days each week, I'd walk to my office, cursing at the men who said "hello" and "bitch" so rapidly the two words seemed like one. I'd get drunk at lunch with writers, then work until nine or ten at night. Home at last, I'd remove the dust wrapped like leather strips inside my fan, explaining to my new kitten that just because *I* was too tired to eat did not mean that she was excused from her dinner.

On other days that summer, I would become very tired at my desk. I would feel inexplicably like crying and so I would leave, walking as if in a trance to Duane Reade Drugs. For an hour, surrounded by other young women in trances, I would pull products off the shelves, arranging them in a blue basket, debating whether or not I needed the nail clippers or perhaps the flashlight batteries. When a Neil Diamond song came on the PA system or the song "If" by Bread, I would stand by the vitamins and cry. I'd tell myself, Perhaps you're premenstrual or, Perhaps you should just let the girls from Beauty analyze your skin type. Eventually I would buy the nail clippers, some sugar cookies in a Christmasy blue tin, and walk back through the revolving doors and to my office.

One day that August, my mother announced that she planned to clean out every inch of the house, including the closet in my bedroom. This I had avoided for years, the way I'd once avoided writing letters to Nanny Etta. But my mother said, "May I remind you that it's nine years since high school?" I told her that I kept track, checked my datebook for an appropriate time, then rode the train out the following Saturday.

I walked from the station, cutting past the old Mays, down to the secret path that led to the park and community pools. My parents, when I arrived, were not at home. I ate nervously from the cookie pile on the dishwasher, then walked downstairs to look around.

In my father's workroom, I studied a picture of us crammed inside a Woolworth's booth the year we had the white furry hats with pom-pom strings. There was Gwyn's tiny handprint

in a silver cement circle; a rock onto which I'd glued strips of
yellow felt; a picture of Sashi in *Godspell.* There was the painting of Franklin D. Roosevelt and in an upright stand, a file
folder marked "Betsy."

It was thick, filled with copies of nearly every article I'd
written, copies of the college paper I'd edited, and beneath it
all, one yellowing copy of the *New York Post* from the winter
of 1978. It was old, chipping at the corners like the inner
sleeve of a Beatle record. Smoothing it out, I ran my hand
carefully across Mr. Stein's face. He had not worn his toupee
to the arraignment. He'd kept his eyes down and his lips
looked brown and flat, the way worms had looked sliced
down the center in Science lab. Above his head were the
words "The Alleged Baby Seller."

Mr. Stein, it seemed, had been accused, in a 192-count
indictment, of selling twenty-four babies to twenty-three
couples over a three-year period for a total of $173,136. Au-
thorities believed that he had placed scouts as far off as Loui-
siana in search of pregnant teens. They also believed that he
had falsified court documents in the ensuing adoptions,
meaning that some of the mothers might have sued and suc-
cessfully gotten back their babies. I read the story all the way
through and the last three paragraphs very carefully. They
said:

> While the babies were sold after birth for from $3,500
> to $10,500, officials said the women who surrendered
> them were given nothing except prenatal shelter, spending
> money, clothing and medical care.
>
> "They were exploited through their own feelings of
> guilt," said one investigator.
>
> "They were told they could have their babies and that
> they could be assured the babies would go to good homes
> and they would never have to feel guilty."

Dropping the paper, I said, "I didn't even get the spending money."

Upstairs in my room, I tried to fluff up the beanbag chair, but it slithered to the floor in a wheezing heap of vinyl. I sighed and sat down alongside it, listening to my father's car pull into the driveway and stop. I heard him go down into his workroom. Two minutes later he stood at my door holding the *Post,* little newspaper chips raining down onto the old pink shag rug.

"Welcome," he said, putting down the paper and lighting his pipe. "Glad you could make it. Glad, too, you decided to look at the old Stein thing. You know, I'd always felt that your refusal to discuss this would break down after a suitable length of time had passed. Perhaps this is the time?"

To rule out any possibility that it was not, my father sat down on the bed and started talking. "Look, Bets," he said. "The Stein escapade shouldn't upset you. Frankly, I don't know whether or not we were involved. But even if we were, think a minute: What exactly would that have meant?"

I was going to answer but he went on. "Okay, try to remember. We were in a very bad situation—financially, emotionally. Now here was a guy who offered us the opportunity to have the whole thing taken care of, cleanly, neatly, on behalf of people who had the money, who were comfortable enough to pay for that kind of service. At worst, you can say that old Larry was a greedy son of a bitch, but that's about it. I'm sure no harm, in any case, came to our child."

"How do you know?" I asked.

"Okay," my father said, sucking on the pipe, which had gone out. "There's something I never told you. But now I'll tell you because perhaps at this point in your life you need to know."

I was sorry I had asked. Taking a deep breath, I said, "Oh, really, what?"

He looked at me, removed the pipe from his mouth and said, "The night we came to fetch you at the hospital, I drove around to check on that couple. I was sure as hell going to see who they were."

"How could you tell it was them?"

"Well, it was dark out. There was only one car parked in that part of the lot."

"What do you mean? It was day. It was scorchingly hot."

"Betsy, it was nine o'clock at night. You weren't in any state to say what time it was."

I was shocked but managed to say, "Who were they?"

"They had the light on in the car, so I got a glimpse. The husband was a pudgy guy, late thirties—wedding band, hands gripping the steering wheel. Next to him sat a well-appointed older woman, a mother-in-law, I guessed. In the backseat a woman waited with blankets and a bottle. She had dark hair. Short bob kind of cut. She looked, in a word, terrified."

"What did they say?"

My father shrugged and tried again to light his pipe. "They said nothing. I don't think they had an idea in hell who I was. I just nodded, said, 'All right,' then drove around to get you, Mommy and Sash."

I attempted to determine what my true feelings were. As far as I could make out, I wanted to kill the woman waiting with her smug little yuppie blankets, stealing someone else's baby because she couldn't come up with her own. But this was clearly irrational.

"Well," my father said, his pipe lit at last. "It's past. Your past. Our past as a family." He laughed. "The only thing we can't ever be rid of, it seems, is the hideous pink in this room—the psycho-pink, or whatever you called it. I remember when I went in to get it made up the guy couldn't believe that this was really what I wanted. He kept asking,

'Now, you're sure about this?' I should go over and tell him what a good job he did. Fifteen years later, Mommy paints over it again and again and it still shows through."

I sat there wiping my hands on the beanbag, although they were sweaty and slid right off. My father's smile faded. "To tell you the truth, Betsy," he said, "if we'd locked you in your mod little pink cave, you would have crawled out the window. There were times I was tempted, but you were beyond control. There was simply no way to do it."

The following Monday was extremely hot for early September. I woke up feeling dizzy, took the subway one stop, got off because I could not breathe and walked. Reaching my office, I sat down for ten minutes, got up and walked back out past Jennifer, my assistant, who was discussing with other assistants someone she'd recently seen in a nightclub bathroom. I continued to walk the forty blocks to my house, and then the seven to Beth Israel emergency. Both arms and legs were numb. My chest ached. According to an ad I'd read earlier on the R train, I was having a heart attack.

After waiting five hours, I learned that I was not having a heart attack. I was diagnosed as nervous and depressed and was sent home to rest. Still I felt ill. I submitted later that week to an EKG and several blood tests and, at my cardiologist's suggestion, agreed to wear a monitor attached to my chest for ten days. I woke up every night of the ten out of breath, sweating, afraid that I was seriously ill. I called doctors I had met and got their services. I called my mother, who said, "Call Donnie, your cousin, immediately. He's a doctor, remember?" I called fake-Cousin Donnie. He said, "You seem to be experiencing nonspecific symptoms." I said, "I can't breathe. How specific can you get?", hung up and called my mother, who said, "All right. I'm having your father drive in this second." I said no, that I was truly better, hung up and called Gwyn. "Sis," she said, yawning, "you just keep taking life too goddamned seriously. Tomorrow, because you need it, I want you to go out and get a perm."

I did not get a perm the next day but walked quickly to work, stopping only when I had reached Jennifer's desk. I leaned against it a moment, trying to recall the things I had planned for that morning. Jennifer leaned over and touched the case at my waist that held the heart monitor. "Is this an Italian bag?" she asked. I excused myself and lay on the floor of my office. Half an hour later Jennifer knocked. I had already missed seventeen calls, she announced, five from Production. Captions were due and they needed a title on "When Love Kills" and cuts from "What If He Slept with Your Soulmate?" Jennifer paused, then added, "'White-Collar Jesus Freaks' was bumped. We're pushing up 'Incest, Ten Years Later, One Daughter Speaks.'"

I groaned at this, rolled up, and when the next call came arranged myself in the chair to speak. It was a former colleague who now worked at *The Times*. She said that an old friend of hers was coming in from California. He was a lawyer and a musician and now a screenwriter. She'd known him for years, and I would love him.

"What are you talking about?" I asked her.

"A date, sweetie," she said, "I want you to go on a date."

I considered this. I had never, technically, been on a date.

The following Saturday I sat in an Ethiopian restaurant telling the lawyer that I was ill—with nonspecific symptoms —and that I could not possibly stay out past 10:00 P.M. Then I told him in some detail what the symptoms were and he listened. At 9:47, as we stood in my vestibule, he said, "I don't know if I should kiss you goodnight or give you a bill." Then he told me that he had business in London over the weekend and asked me to go with him. Playing with a piece of metal that hung from my mailbox, I said that I couldn't. I was too ill, too fucked up, I didn't have the right clothes.

"I am twenty-six years old," I said, bursting into tears as if I'd waited weeks for just this moment. "I am twenty-six and I am a publishing executive but I jump around my apartment to old Beatle records. I am not a well person."

The lawyer yanked off the piece of metal. "So, at least it's not Gerry and the Pacemakers," he said, shrugging. "Let's go to London anyway."

I did not go to London and the following week turned twenty-seven. At a vegetarian restaurant on lower Broadway, seated across from my parents, I started crying again and could not stop. I cried for so long that we had to leave without eating. Back in my apartment I walked in circles, kicking dust configurations the size of teacups into corners. My parents watched.

"Why don't you open your presents?" asked my mother.

They had brought me drinking glasses, an ironing board and silverware. It was a good start, my mother said, and maybe soon I'd want to work on the furniture. We cut the cake. Friends called and spoke to the answering machine. Listening, I curled up on the rug with my cat. It was warm on the floor. I took the opportunity to fall asleep. When I woke up it turned out that my parents were still there, watching. My father shook a finger at me.

"Now, you listen," he said, "and you listen good. It's about time you cut the crap and pulled things together in this dramatic mush you call a life, do you hear what I'm saying?" I sat up. "Okay," he went on, "so you're a big success, a whiz kid publishing star. But there is goddamned more to life than work and continual exhaustion. Now, it seems to me that you have some serious questions to ask yourself, and it's time you started asking them. You are twenty-seven years old now. This cannot go on."

238 • B E T S Y I S R A E L

My mother kneeled at my side to brush the back of my hair, which I had missed. "You girls were always in such a hurry about everything," she said, sighing. "When you're grown up fast like that, I think at some point it just catches up with you."

We sat there a while longer. Finally my father stood and walked to the door. "Figure out what those questions are," he said as he jiggled the police lock. "Get help if you need it, but find those answers, and do it now! Get on with your freaking life!"

He was out the door.

"Happy birthday, sweetheart," my mother said. "You'll figure things out soon." She kissed me, took the cake plate and followed him out down the stairs.

One morning in October, on the first real day of fall, I got a call from the lawyer, who'd gone to London by himself. I said that I was feeling better. He said, "Does that mean that *a)* you're no longer leaping about to Beatle albums? and *b)* that you'll come visit me?" I said, "No, I am," and, "Yes, I will," although I was not yet entirely better. I had not asked or answered any questions and would not until one afternoon in December, on a lunch break in midtown, some clue about things worked its way up my throat and burst out in the sound of *oh* at the way three people looked from a distance.

If they had turned around that afternoon—the father, the mother, the girl in the purple coat—they would have seen only this: a frantic twenty-seven-year-old woman wearing a black trench coat that lacked buttons and had a coffee stain like a stripe on its sleeve. They might have noticed drool on the chin. They might have looked around for a cop.

I might have looked, just for a second, through a window onto the past as it flew up with a crash and then fell, the last sound in a dream you remember forever. But it was not quite that romantic. I told Ashley, who was gripping my arm, "I thought I saw some people I knew a long time ago, but probably not. And the truth is, of course, that even if I had seen them, if I'd somehow been sure it was them, I would not really have known them at all. What exists, what haunts, is in my head."

Ashley released my arm, said, "So *you* write 'The Relationship That Wouldn't Die,'" and walked off to do his errands. I held my coat closed and walked along Madison Avenue back to my office.

If I hurried, there would be time to write something down before dark.

ACKNOWLEDGMENTS

The following people contributed to the writing of this book:

I am especially grateful to my agent, Melanie Jackson, and to my editor, Ann Patty, who understood before I did how—and why—this book should be written.

Stacy Schiff at Poseidon offered invaluable guidance in the shaping and editing of the manuscript.

For their reading of *Grown-Up Fast* as a work in progress, I am indebted to Kathy Rich, Marilyn Johnson and Lee Lusardi. And for their early encouragement, patient listening and general enthusiasm, I am grateful to Nan Friedman, David Hirshey, Cathryn Jakobson, Mrs. Deborah Margolis, Cheryl Smith, Robin Towner and the articles staff of *Mademoiselle* magazine.

Finally, this book could not have been coherently written without the inexhaustible patience, good cooking skills and incisive legal advice of Ezra J. Doner.